Relational–Cultural Therapy
Second Edition

Theories of Psychotherapy Series

Person-Centered Psychotherapies
   David J. Cain

Psychoanalysis and Psychoanalytic Therapies
   Jeremy D. Safran

Psychotherapy Case Formulation
   Tracy D. Eells

Psychotherapy Integration
   George Stricker

Rational Emotive Behavior Therapy
   Albert Ellis and Debbie Joffe Ellis

Reality Therapy
   Robert E. Wubbolding

Relational–Cultural Therapy, Second Edition
   Judith V. Jordan

Theories of Psychotherapy Series

Jon Carlson and Matt Englar-Carlson, Series Editors

Relational–Cultural Therapy

Second Edition

Judith V. Jordan

American Psychological Association

Washington, DC

Published by
American Psychological Association
750 First Street, NE
Washington, DC 20002
www.apa.org

APA Order Department
P.O. Box 92984
Washington, DC 20090-2984
Phone: (800) 374-2721; Direct: (202) 336-5510
Fax: (202) 336-5502; TDD/TTY: (202) 336-6123
Online: www.apa.org/pubs/books
E-mail: order@apa.org

In the U.K., Europe, Africa, and the Middle East, copies may be ordered from
Eurospan Group
c/o Pegasus Drive
Stratton Business Park
Biggleswade Bedfordshire
SG18 8TQ United Kingdom
Phone: +44 (0) 1767 604972
Fax: +44 (0) 1767 601640
Online: https://www.eurospanbookstore.com/apa
E-mail: eurospan@turpin-distribution.com

Typeset in Minion by Circle Graphics, Inc., Columbia, MD

Printer: Gasch Printing, Odenton, MD
Cover Designer: Minker Design, Sarasota, FL
Cover Art: *Lily Rising*, 2005, oil and mixed media on panel in craquelure frame, by Betsy Bauer

Library of Congress Cataloging-in-Publication Data
Names: Jordan, Judith V., author.
Title: Relational–cultural therapy / Judith V. Jordan.
Description: Second edition. | Washington, DC : American Psychological
   Association, [2018] | Series: Theories of psychotherapy | Includes
   bibliographical references and index.
Identifiers: LCCN 2017022225 | ISBN 9781433828263 | ISBN 143382826X
Subjects: LCSH: Eclectic psychotherapy. | Cultural psychiatry.
Classification: LCC RC554 .J67 2018 | DDC 616.89/14—dc23 LC record available at
   https://lccn.loc.gov/2017022225

British Library Cataloguing-in-Publication Data
A CIP record is available from the British Library.

Printed in the United States of America
Second Edition

http://dx.doi.org/10.1037/0000063-000

10 9 8 7 6 5 4

Contents

Series Preface

S ome might argue that in the contemporary clinical practice of psychotherapy, evidence-based intervention and effective outcome have overshadowed theory in importance. Maybe. But, as the editors of this series, we don't propose to take up that controversy here. We do know that psychotherapists adopt and practice according to one theory or another because their experience, and decades of good evidence, suggest that having a sound theory of psychotherapy leads to greater therapeutic success. Still, the role of theory in the helping process can be hard to explain. This narrative about solving problems helps convey theory's importance:

> Aesop tells the fable of the sun and wind having a contest to decide who was the most powerful. From above the earth, they spotted a man walking down the street, and the wind said that he bet he could get his coat off. The sun agreed to the contest. The wind blew, and the man held on tightly to his coat. The more the wind blew, the tighter he held. The sun said it was his turn. He put all of his energy into creating warm sunshine, and soon the man took off his coat.

What does a competition between the sun and the wind to remove a man's coat have to do with theories of psychotherapy? We think this deceptively simple story highlights the importance of theory as the precursor to any effective intervention—and hence to a favorable outcome. Without a guiding theory we might treat the symptom without understanding the role of the individual. Or we might create power conflicts with our clients and not understand that, at times, indirect means of helping (sunshine) are often as effective—if not more so—than direct ones (wind). In the absence of theory, we might lose track of the treatment rationale and instead get caught up in, for example, social correctness and not wanting to do something that looks too simple.

What exactly *is* theory? The *APA Dictionary of Psychology, Second Edition* defines theory as "a principle or body of interrelated principles that purports to explain or predict a number of interrelated phenomena" (VandenBos, 2015, p. 1081). In psychotherapy, a theory is a set of principles used to explain human thought and behavior, including what causes people to change. In practice, a theory creates the goals of therapy and specifies how to pursue them. Haley (1997) noted that a theory of psychotherapy ought to be simple enough for the average therapist to understand, but comprehensive enough to account for a wide range of eventualities. Furthermore, a theory guides action toward successful outcomes while generating hope in both the therapist and client that recovery is possible.

Theory is the compass that allows psychotherapists to navigate the vast territory of clinical practice. In the same ways that navigational tools have been modified to adapt to advances in thinking and ever-expanding territories to explore, theories of psychotherapy have changed over time. The different schools of theories are commonly referred to as waves, the first wave being psychodynamic theories (i.e., Adlerian, psychoanalytic), the second wave learning theories (i.e., behavioral, cognitive–behavioral), the third wave humanistic theories (person-centered, gestalt, existential), the fourth wave feminist and multicultural theories, and the fifth wave postmodern and constructivist theories (i.e., narrative, solution-focused). In many ways, these waves represent how psychotherapy has adapted and responded to changes in psychology, society, and epistemology as well as to changes in the nature of psychotherapy itself. Psychotherapy and the theories that guide it are dynamic and responsive. The wide variety of theories is also testament to the different ways in which the same human behavior can be conceptualized (Frew & Spiegler, 2012).

It is with these two concepts in mind—the central importance of theory and the natural evolution of theoretical thinking—that we developed the American Psychological Association (APA) Theories of Psychotherapy

Series. Both of us are thoroughly fascinated by theory and the range of complex ideas that drive each model. As university faculty members who teach courses on the theories of psychotherapy, we wanted to create learning materials that not only highlight the essence of the major theories for professionals and professionals-in-training but also clearly bring the reader up to date on the current status of the models. Often in books on theory, the biography of the original theorist overshadows the evolution of the model. In contrast, our intent is to highlight the contemporary uses of the theories as well as their history and context. Further, we wanted each theory to be reflected through the process of working with clients that reflect the full range of human diversity.

As this project began, we faced two immediate decisions: which theories to address and who best to present them. We looked at graduate-level theories of psychotherapy courses to see which theories are being taught, and we explored popular scholarly books, articles, and conferences to determine which theories draw the most interest. We then developed a dream list of authors from among the best minds in contemporary theoretical practice. Each author is one of the leading proponents of that approach as well as a knowledgeable practitioner. We asked each author to review the core constructs of the theory, bring the theory into the modern sphere of clinical practice by looking at it in the context of evidence-based practice, and clearly illustrate how the theory looks in action.

Each title in the series can stand alone or be grouped together with other titles to create materials for a course in psychotherapy theories. This option allows instructors to create a course featuring the approaches they believe are the most salient today. To support this end, APA Books has also developed a DVD for most of the approaches that demonstrates the theory in practice with a real client. Many of the DVDs show therapy over six sessions. For a complete list of available DVD programs, visit the APA website (http://www.apa.org/pubs/videos).

In this second edition, Judith V. Jordan clearly describes relational–cultural theory (RCT) and how it guides an effective psychological practice. As a more recently developed theory of psychotherapy, RCT draws on aspects of psychodynamic and feminist theory in developing a relational model that emphasizes the primacy of human connection and relationships. Another unique aspect is that most of the developers of RCT were women, and the model specifically considers the influence of culture and identity in developing relationships both inside and outside of psychotherapy. RCT is clearly a theoretical approach for modern times as it is consistent with scientific advances in neuroscience and societal focuses in psychology on social justice issues. Dr. Jordan draws on her own knowledge as one of the original theorists of this approach, on her vast experience as a practicing psychotherapist, and on her work as director of Wellesley College's Jean Baker Miller Training Institute. The numerous case studies will help readers to gain familiarity with the theory by reading about it in practice. This edition provides further information on RCT advances in clinical practice and new areas of application. We were especially pleased to present the first edition of this book because it represented the first complete review of RCT. With this second edition, readers can see new advances in RCT as the approach has developed a broader evidence base in the field of psychotherapy. Thus, this edition represents another milestone in the evolution of this important theory.

—Jon Carlson and Matt Englar-Carlson

How to Use This Book With APA Psychotherapy Videos

Each book in the Theories of Psychotherapy Series is specifically paired with a DVD that demonstrates the theory applied in actual therapy with a real client. Many DVDs feature the author of the book as the guest therapist, allowing students to see an eminent scholar and practitioner putting the theory they write about into action.

The DVDs have a number of features that make them excellent tools for learning more about theoretical concepts:

- Many DVDs contain six full sessions of psychotherapy over time, giving viewers a chance to see how clients respond to the application of the theory over the course of several sessions.
- Each DVD has a brief introductory discussion recapping the basic features of the theory behind the approach demonstrated. This allows viewers to review the key aspects of the approach about which they have just read.
- DVDs feature actual clients in unedited psychotherapy sessions. This provides a unique opportunity to get a sense of the look and feel of real psychotherapy, something that written case examples and transcripts sometimes cannot convey.
- There is a therapist commentary track that viewers may choose to play during the psychotherapy sessions. This track gives unique insight into why therapists do what they do in a session. Further it provides an in vivo opportunity to see how the therapist uses the model to concep-tualize the client.

The books and DVDs together make a powerful teaching tool for showing how theoretical principles affect practice. In the case of this book, the DVD *Relational–Cultural Therapy*, which features the author as the guest expert, provides a vivid example of how this approach looks in practice.

Relational–Cultural Therapy

Second Edition

1

Introduction

Mainstream Western psychological theories tend to depict human development as a trajectory from dependence to independence. In these models, the "job" of parenting is to bring the dependent, helpless baby into a state of autonomous and independent adulthood. In contrast, relational–cultural theory (RCT) is built on the premise that, throughout the lifespan, human beings grow through and toward connection. It holds that we need connections to flourish, even to stay alive, and isolation is a major source of suffering for people, at both a personal and cultural level. Seeing connection as the primary ongoing organizer and source of motivation in people's lives transforms the work of socialization into assisting our children to develop relational skills and to elaborate the possibility for mutuality in relationships. It furthermore calls attention to the need to alter the sociopolitical forces of disconnection that create significant pain for people. Invested in the task of social change, RCT provides a model for

http://dx.doi.org/10.1037/0000063-001
Relational–Cultural Therapy, Second Edition, by J. V. Jordan

doing therapy that emphasizes movement out of isolation (Banks, 2016; Jordan, 2017; M. Walker, 2008b). RCT challenges not only the prevailing developmental theories, which frame independence as the hallmark of mature development, but also some of the basic tenets of 21st-century Western culture, which celebrate autonomy, self-interest, competition, and strength in isolation.

Relational psychology is rooted in the tenet that we grow through and toward relationship throughout the lifespan and that we need relationships in the same, life-sustaining ways that we need air and water. We are simply and essentially interdependent beings; we need a culture that supports rather than demeans our need for others. When we overemphasize a goal of autonomy and "standing on your own," we are siding against our own neurobiology. We create chronic stress. Honoring our relational nature allows us to reach out for comfort when we are afraid or to seek others' viewpoints when we are working on a project. We appreciate the many ways that mutual connection contributes to creativity.

Although initially ignored then treated as "dangerous," RCT theory and practice have influenced many theoretical approaches. Now many of those who initially resisted RCT have increasingly assimilated much of the relational model and suggest that "we knew this all along." The ideas are becoming more mainstream, and significant research is being carried out to test various aspects and applications of RCT (Comstock, 2005; Duffey & Trepal, 2016; Frey, 2013; Lenz, 2016; Norcross, 2002; Oakley et al., 2013; Tantillo & Sanftner, 2010b). Some have applied it to areas other than clinical practice and counseling (Schwartz & Holloway, 2012; Spencer & Liang, 2009). As Robb (2006) noted, to study relationships rather than selves "changes everything." Although RCT initially evolved in the context of better understanding the psychology of women, it now acknowledges the need for better understanding boys and men as well. RCT posits that all people need to participate in relationships that foster growth; models of human development that emphasize only self-interest and autonomy are not only inaccurate but create suffering. We are wired to flourish in connection, but our culture pushes us to stand separate and compete with one another. This dilemma and clash generate chronic stress and disconnection. The message of healing connections and an appreciation of our primary yearning for connection has resonated with many clinicians, students, educators, and policymakers. There is burgeoning interest in RCT among graduate students, and many doctoral dissertations have used RCT as their theoretical lens. The first edition of *Relational–Cultural Therapy* (Jordan, 2010) is used in many graduate programs, and the theory has also been represented in college texts (e.g., Engler, 2006; Frager & Fadiman, 2013; Ivey, D'Andrea, Ivey, & Simek-Morgan, 2007; Magnavita, 2004).

THE MYTH OF THE SEPARATE SELF *separate self*

Most traditional Western developmental and clinical theories are built on a core belief in the importance of the growth of the *separate self*. Thus, autonomy, individuation, firm self-boundaries, separation, and the increasing use of logical, abstract thought are seen as markers of maturity. The ascendance of thought over emotion, the importance of being able to separate thought from emotion, is celebrated. The cultural values of individualism, of "standing on your own two feet," and competing with others to attain your best performance infuse many of the so-called value-free scientific psychological paradigms.

Several biases have prominently shaped clinical-developmental theories about the self. In its attempt to establish itself as a bona fide "hard science," the young discipline of psychology modeled itself after Newtonian physics (Jordan, 2000), which is "rooted in Baconian models of science, [and] emphasizes the primary separateness of objects" (Jordan, 2001, p. 92). Newtonian physics posited discrete, separate entities existing in space and acting on each other in predictable and measurable ways. This easily led to a study of the self as a comparably bounded and contained "molecular" entity, a notion most visibly supported by the existence of separate body identities (Jordan, Kaplan, Miller, Stiver, & Surrey, 1991).

Although it has often been presented as a natural fact, *the self* is actually a construct. It is based on a spatial metaphor: The self is seen as occupying space and characterized by a center and a containing wall (Cooley, 1902/1968). In most models, it is portrayed as functioning best if it has a strong, containing boundary protecting it from the potentially dangerous surrounding context. Self-protection and self-coherence are seen as major functions of the self (Kohut, 1984). In most psychodynamic theories, the self is seen as functioning better if it is more independent of other selves. Better yet is a self that has power over other selves and has no need of others. The biases of psychological self-sufficiency run deep. In the separate-self model, the myth of independence comes to obscure the inevitable dependence and interconnectedness of human beings. Markus and Kitayama (1991) noted that "achieving the cultural goal of independence requires construction of oneself as an individual whose behavior is organized and made meaningful primarily by reference to one's own internal repertoire of thoughts, feelings and actions" (p. 226).

In Western industrialized nations, the self is encouraged to be mobile and free of constraining bonds of community. It is competitive and achieves safety and a sense of well-being by successfully competing with and beating others. Gaining ascendant power over others is seen as the route to safety and maturity. These myths of development are seen as universal, but they are especially enforced in dominant Western socialization of young boys (Pollack, 1998). Although many young boys and men are injured by the expectations for autonomy and hyperindividualism, many men are privileged with power and status when they achieve some semblance of competitive success. Making invisible their dependencies on others to achieve this, they falsely claim that they have earned their advantage on their own. But for both sexes the expectation of unrealizable goals of independence and invulnerability lead to great stress and even poor physical health.

FUNDAMENTAL PRINCIPLES OF RCT

The practice of RCT is based on a new model of human development that places connection at the center of growth. The fundamental principles of RCT, as it emerged over the years, posit that we grow in relationship throughout our lives. RCT sees the ideal of psychological separation as illusory and defeating because the human condition is one of inevitable interdependence throughout the lifespan. Increasing relationship differentiation, rather than separation from sustaining relationships, is the route of development (Jordan et al., 1991; Surrey, 1991). The theory does not propose step-wise, "fixed" states or unidirectional paths of development. Instead, it points to increasing levels of complexity and articulation within relationships with an increasing capacity for mutuality.

Growth-fostering relationships are characterized by (a) zest; an increase in energy; (b) increased knowledge and clarity about one's own experience, the other person, and the relationship; (c) creativity and productivity; (d) a greater sense of worth; and (e) a desire for more connection (Miller & Stiver, 1997). Development involves increasing elaboration and differentiation of relational patterns and capacities (Miller & Stiver, 1997). Human beings seek to participate in relationships in which people both give and receive. The ideal movement is toward authenticity, mutual empathy, and mutual empowerment. Empathy, a complex cognitive and affective capacity, fuels this movement because it is at the heart of our sense of resonance and responsiveness to others. Indeed, although empathy evolves with complexity and nuance throughout the lifespan, we are neurologically hardwired to connect with others (Banks, 2016; Eisenberger & Lieberman, 2004); babies come into the world with a strong readiness to be responsive to other human beings, crying in response to the distress cries of other infants (Sagi & Hoffman, 1976; Simner, 1971).

Mutual empathy, a concept first articulated within the RCT model in 1981 (Jordan, 1986), suggests that for empathy to facilitate change, each person must see, know, and feel the responsiveness of the other person. Mutual empathy involves mutual impact, mutual care, and mutual responsiveness. It contributes to repair of empathic failures and alters relational expectations created in early formative relationships. This concept is fundamental to the therapeutic practice of RCT. Simply put, therapy involves a dance of responsiveness: The therapist says to the client, in effect, "I empathize with you, with your experience and pain, and I am letting you see that your pain has affected me and you matter to me." The client sees, knows, and feels (or empathizes with) the therapist's empathy and thereby begins to experience a sense of relational competence and efficacy (Jordan, 2000). In this context, the client finds and experiences the ability to create a caring response in the other person at the same time as her or his sense of isolation diminishes. Both client and therapist begin to move into growth-fostering connection (Jordan, 2000, 2002), which in turn facilitates the client's broader movement from disconnection to reconnection. Where "stuckness" prevailed, psychological movement and growth begin.

RCT should not be misconstrued as a compendium of harmonious and cozy relationships. Founder Jean Baker Miller argued strongly that "good conflict" is necessary for change and growth, and she suggested that we undergo our most profound change and grow most deeply when we encounter difference and work on conflict or differences in connection. For Miller, conflict is not defined by dominance, violence, or aggression; rather, these modes of interaction are seen as maneuvers to avoid conflict and change. Working with conflict and difference in therapy becomes crucial. The therapist cannot withdraw into a position of power, distance, or all-knowing objectivity. Instead, the therapist must be present with the differences that arise and open to admitting and learning from his or her contribution to the conflict or disconnections that ensue from the interactions.

This quality of responsive presence on the part of the therapist is one of the defining features of RCT therapy. RCT therapy is based largely on a change in attitude and understanding rather than a set of techniques. RCT practitioners believe that clients are worthy of profound respect and that therapy involves an openness to change on the part of both, or all, participants. This attitude of mutuality underlies the practice of mutual empathy and mutual empowerment, the cornerstones of RCT models of change and growth.

DIFFERENCES, STRATIFICATION, AND PRIVILEGE

If connection is the goal of RCT, disconnection is the challenge it seeks to overcome. Acute disconnections occur in all relationships and by themselves are not harmful. If they are reworked in a way that allows both people to feel respected and effective, acute disconnections can enable growth of trust and positive expectations for relationships. Chronic disconnections, on the other hand, are the source of what most people call *pathology* and result from repeatedly encountering nonempathic responses. At the extreme, they result from humiliations, violations, abuse, and emotional neglect. More traditional therapists sometimes focus on the ways that chronic disconnections create hopelessness and isolation on a personal level; RCT also points to the ways in which disconnections created by stratified social organization and marginalization contribute to the experience of immobilization and isolation. Racism, homophobia, class prejudice, and sexism all lead to chronic disconnections that create pain and drain energy in individuals and societies. Few clinical theories have paid attention to the suffering caused by existing societal power arrangements. An exception was noted by Miller (1973): "Alfred Adler was the first psychoanalyst to condemn society's conception of women and to see this conception, in itself, as a root contributing cause of the psychological problems not only of women but also of women and children" (p. 3). Analyzing the impact of dominance and subordination on groups and individuals—including, but not limited to, women—is a key aspect of the social justice agenda of RCT (Miller, 1986).

To express authentic feelings, one must enjoy sufficient safety to be vulnerable; this is directly related to how much mutuality exists in a relationship. Privilege and marginalization arise around the stratification of differences in this culture. The dominant culture distorts images of self, images of other, and images of relational possibilities in ways that impede mutuality (Ayvazian & Tatum, 1994; M. Walker & Miller, 2000). RCT seeks to help individuals expand and resist the constricting nature of these relational and controlling images.

Some theorists treat issues of privilege and the effects of dominance and social injustice as irrelevant to theory building, developmental theories, and/or the practice of clinical psychology. Others see these issues as peripheral—"add-ons" incorporated to be politically correct or pay lip service to cultural competence. RCT suggests that issues of power imbalance and oppression are central to any therapeutic understanding and intervention. Unacknowledged privilege and the subtle or blatant use of power over others inevitably create division, anger, disempowerment, depression, shame, and disconnection.

Relationships are embedded in culture. Theory is embedded in culture as well. Psychology theorists have a responsibility to recognize the biases and value structures that inform their theories. Without this recognition, theory is passed off as "objective," and the interests it serves remain invisible: "The history of psychological theory is replete with evidence of complicity with cultural arrangements and power practices that divide people into groups of dominants and subordinates" (Jordan & Walker, 2004, p. 3). RCT maintains that understanding the culture and its distortions is essential to understanding the individual who lives within or on the periphery of that culture: "To place culture, alongside connection, at the center of the theory is to break a critical silence. First it acknowledges that social and political values inform theories of human psychology, including those that valorize separation and autonomy" (Jordan & Walker, 2004, p. 3).

The illusion of separation and the celebration of autonomy are part of the denial or denigration of our basic need to participate in growth-fostering relationships. Western culture valorizes these disconnected individualistic qualities. In such a culture, people with privilege can falsely appear more self-sufficient, more mature, more worthy of the privilege. But evidence increasingly suggests that people need to contribute to the growth of others and experience others' willingness to engage in mutually beneficial interactions. To address these needs effectively, therapists need to ask: How has psychology been complicit in building cultural values that embrace separation and independence? How have psychology and clinical practice been shaped by, but also created and sustained, a culture of disconnection? How has psychology helped to sustain a culture of privilege and prejudice?

These questions themselves contribute to the possibility of achieving social justice and dispel the illusion of the objectivity and neutrality of any theoretical position. In addressing them, RCT acknowledges its value biases: the belief that the capacity to build good connection is an essential human skill; the belief that it is valuable, even essential, for our global well-being that human beings develop relational skills and honor our basic need for connection; the belief that people have an *essential* need to connect with others; the belief that if these core yearnings for connection are supported by the larger context and people learn how to relate in growth-fostering ways with one another, people will experience an increasing sense of well-being at a personal and collective level.

2

History

If we want to locate a single origin point for relational–cultural theory (RCT), it would have to be psychiatrist Jean Baker Miller's (1976) ground-breaking book, _Toward a New Psychology of Women_. Miller examined what had been considered women's weaknesses and argued that they could be construed as strengths. She began to deconstruct the supposedly "neutral" psychology of the individual and proposed instead that hidden forces of power and dominance play a major role in shaping social and individual development. Miller placed relationships at the center of growth and questioned the usefulness of the concept of self (specifically the _separate self_) in understanding women, suggesting that women are the "carriers," for all people, of the basic need for human connection throughout the lifespan. RCT emerged out of these insights, coupled with psychodynamic models of therapy and reframed, as the years passed, by new thinking on race, difference, and social justice.

http://dx.doi.org/10.1037/0000063-002
Relational–Cultural Therapy, Second Edition, by J. V. Jordan
Copyright © 2018 by the American Psychological Association. All rights reserved.

THE FEMINIST AND SOCIAL JUSTICE ROOTS OF RCT

In 1978, Miller began to work with three psychologists, Irene Stiver, Judith Jordan, and Janet Surrey, to critique the ways in which traditional psychodynamic theories misrepresented women's experience. Their collaborative efforts, originally known as the Stone Center theory and self-in-relation theory, generated the body of work that comprises RCT. Discussing their clinical cases and listening to the voices of their female clients, the four women further explored the limitations of what had been put forward as a psychology of *all* human beings. Beginning in 1981, this collaborative group began to write and present their ideas at psychological and academic conferences in the United States and Canada.

When Miller was made the first director of the Stone Center for Developmental Studies and Services at Wellesley College, the group found an institutional home. The Stone Center was inaugurated in 1981 when the Stone family generously endowed a center for the study of mental health and the prevention of mental illness. As its first director, Miller framed the accurate representation of women's psychological development as a major contribution to positive health for women. The establishment of a colloquium series led to publication of the Stone Center Works in Progress. Over the succeeding years, this group published more than 100 works in progress and more than 20 books (Jordan, 1997, 2000, 2010; Jordan, Kaplan, Miller, Stiver, & Surrey, 1991; Miller, 1985; Miller & Stiver, 1997; Robb, 2006; Shem & Surrey, 1998; M. Walker, 2011; M. Walker & Rosen, 2004; see Suggested Readings, this volume, for a complete listing). Although not an original member, Alexandra Kaplan joined the group for several years before her premature death from Alzheimer's disease. In the 1980s, several study groups joined the core theory group; these groups represented issues of interest to women of color, lesbians and bisexual women, and women suffering with chronic illness. Maureen Walker, Amy Banks, Wendy Rosen, and Linda Hartling became members of the core theory group. The initial response from traditional theorists was to ignore the insights being put forth by the Stone Center Theory group; later they would label the concepts as dangerous because RCT challenged many long-held assumptions about the therapist's role and the client–therapist relationship. In the end, however, the final response was to say, "We knew this all along." Today there is growing acceptance and assimilation of relational–cultural ideas.

During the same period in which RCT was emerging, independently at Harvard, in a more traditional academic/research setting, Carol Gilligan was raising similar questions about how traditional developmental theories applied to the psychology of women. Noting that Kohlberg's theory of moral development was based entirely on studies of males, Gilligan (1982) questioned the accuracy of applying these standards to girls and women. Instead of a morality of "rights" and abstract principles of justice, Gilligan noted that women were characterized by a morality of "care." When male standards of abstract justice, autonomy, competition, and independence were applied to girls and women, they were seen as deficient, inadequately developed, or less mature than men. In 1987, the RCT theorists, Gilligan and her graduate students (including Annie Rogers and Lyn Brown), and Judith Herman's Victims of Violence group began organizing a conference sponsored by the Harvard Medical School called "Learning From Women." At these meetings, held every other year and attended by 300 to 2,000 people, these three groups shared their new knowledge and understanding, exploring their similarities and differences. Clearly, all three groups struck a note of resonance in the many conference participants over the years.

Early RCT theory was skewed by the fact that the original writers were all White, middle class, and well educated. Although these writers as women protested the distortions imposed mostly by men on a psychology of women, they unfortunately duplicated this distortion by talking about *woman's voice* rather than *women's voices*, revealing how the assumption of universality by the privileged dominant group creeps into even the most conscious attempts to incorporate diversity and appreciate power inequities. Women of color, lesbians, other sexually identified women, physically challenged women, and women from different economic backgrounds personally communicated in conferences, workshops, and Works in Progress that "the theory group" was committing the very distortions of exclusion they were protesting.

In 1976, Jean Baker Miller had substantially explored these issues in *Toward a New Psychology of Women*; they were brought back to the center of the Stone Center work by those groups who felt once again excluded or pushed to the margin. Members of the original group saw the truth in their critique and acknowledged that they were coming from a position of great privilege and unearned advantage with the unchecked assumptions of universality that so often accompany that position (McIntosh, 1980, 1988). This is what bell hooks (1984) referred to as living at "the center" rather than at "the margin." It is not a place that promotes appreciation of difference. Instead, it promotes the exercise of power over others and entitlement in the privileged group. Steps were taken to ensure that the voices of marginalized women were included in the theoretical discussions—not as "add-ons" but as central developers of the model. After 1985, publications from the Stone Center reflect these influences and an evolving emphasis on issues of race, sexual orientation, and societal patterns of dominance and subordination (M. Alvarez, 1995; Coll, Cook-Nobles, & Surrey, 1995; Desai, 1999; Eldridge, Mencher, & Slater, 1993; Jenkins, 1998; Rosen, 1992; Sparks, 1999; Tatum, 1993, 1997; Tatum & Garrick Knaplund, 1996; C. Turner, 1984, 1987; M. Walker, 1999, 2001, 2002a; M. Walker & Miller, 2000; J. V. Ward, 2000). RCT's emphasis on the destructive influence of "power over" relationships and the stratification of society around power imbalances also deepened (Cholewa, Goodman, West-Olatunji, & Amatea, 2014; Jordan, Walker, & Hartling, 2004; Miller, 2003; M. Walker, 2002b).

RCT has increasingly moved toward trying to represent women's (and men's) many voices as they are shaped not only by early caretakers but also by sociopolitical, racial, cultural, sexual, and economic contexts. More recently the delineation of the impact of race, class, sexual orientation, and all types of marginalization on individuals and groups of individuals—both men and women—has been at the center of this work. *Women's Growth in Diversity* (Jordan, 1997) "brought a phenomenological focus to the experience of women whose voices had been historically marginalized from the mainstream" (Jordan & Walker, 2004, p. 3). The inclusion of these voices was intended to challenge assumptions of a powerful mythic norm that would define "woman as a white, economically privileged, able-bodied and heterosexual female. Unchallenged, this norm becomes a standard against which all women's existence is interpreted and evaluated" (Jordan & Walker, 2004, p. 3).

The Jean Baker Miller Training Institute was created in 1995 to further the work of RCT. In the past, the institute conducted trainings twice a year for clinicians and once a year for professionals interested in the application of RCT to organizations and leadership. Joyce Fletcher has focused on the usefulness of RCT in understanding business and organizational models (Fletcher, 1999, 2007; Fletcher, Jordan, & Miller, 2000; Myerson & Fletcher, 2000). More recently, the intensive institutes have brought together several threads of RCT practice: educational, clinical, neurobiological, and social justice aspects. These tracks are bringing forth new applications of RCT. In the past, these trainings were held at Wellesley College, but most recently we have been hosted by groups around the country who have a strong interest in bringing RCT into their communities and practices. Each year, the institute has also conducted special workshops on emerging topics of interest, such as the neurobiology of relationships, relational mindfulness, mothers and sons, mothers and daughters, antiracism work, relational mentoring, new models of leadership, treating eating disorders, and practicing RCT to create social change and contribute to social justice. A research network holds a poster session during our intensive institute to bring people up-to-date on recent RCT research that is being conducted in many regions. Researchers from around the world gather to share their RCT-inspired work. The institute's faculty continues to write and present at conferences despite the demise of two of its prime contributors and visionary leaders: Jean Baker Miller and Irene Stiver. RCT has been featured in college and graduate textbooks, alongside the theories of Freud, Jung, Horney, and other major psychologists and psychoanalysts (Corey, 2009; Engler, 2003; Frager & Fadiman, 1998; Frager & Fadiman, 2013). Outside of the academy, RCT's prominent place in contemporary culture was cemented by Pulitzer Prize–winning journalist Christina Robb's 2006 book, *This Changes Everything: The Relational Revolution in Psychology*. More recently, Banks's (2016) *Wired to Connect* has brought the relational–cultural neurobiology of connection to a wider audience.

THE PSYCHODYNAMIC CONTEXTS OF RCT

The founding scholars of RCT (see Jordan et al., 1991) were all trained in psychoanalytically oriented psychodynamic models. Many concepts from those earlier models have been incorporated into or adapted for RCT. Like other psychodynamic theories, for instance, RCT could be described as a theory and practice that centers on "talk therapy," holds the belief that early and ongoing relationships shape much of a person's life, and endorses the idea that many of the expectations people hold for relationships are not conscious but nevertheless influence our behavior. Although RCT does not typically use the language of transference and countertransference, its concept of relational images—or expectations that generalize from past to present interactions—has much in common with transference. One difference is the emphasis in RCT that these expectations operate not just in the therapy relationship but in all relationships. Despite these similarities, however, there are key points of differentiation between RCT and some of the major psychodynamic theories, including Freudian psychoanalysis, object relations theory, and the work of Stern (1986), Kohut (1984), and Rogers (1951, 1980).

Many people suggest that Freudian theory does not exercise extensive influence in today's therapeutic community. Certainly classical Freudian psychoanalysis has been questioned and modified on many fronts (Safran & Muran, 2000). But it continues to have a pervasive, hidden impact on many modern-day clinical models and on the broader society, infiltrating the culture in ways that are not always immediately visible. Although Freud's theory is not usually thought of as a theory of "self," his model is profoundly intrapsychic in its emphasis on the structures of ego, id, and superego. *Das Ich* (traditionally translated as "ego") is literally "the I," what one could call the subjective and agentic experience of Self. *Das Ich* manages impulses and the conscience. It is internal, separate from context and part of the intrapsychic structure. Freudian theory is biased by a view of people as selfish at the core, driven by libido and aggression. Freud (1920/1955) once commented, "Protection against stimuli is almost more important than reception of stimuli" (p. 27). This registers a powerful emphasis on boundedness. In these traditional models, boundaries keep the organism inside safe; they defend against the impinging and endangering context outside. Seeing the self as endangered in relationship to its surroundings keeps in place the notion that the safest way to live is to be walled off from, more powerful than, and thus protected from others. In contrast, unlike Freud's construction of boundary as a place of resisting intrusion from the outside, RCT sees the boundary as a place of meeting, learning, differentiation, and exchange. It is mutually empathic relationships, not power over others, that provide a sense of safety and motivation toward more connection. Mutual empathy is built on a foundation of trust and responsiveness. In RCT, relationships are central to surviving and thriving. They are essential to supporting life.

Freud (1920/1955) suggested that relationships were secondary to drive satisfaction, piggybacked onto the primary drives like hunger and sex. Object relations theorists attempted to distance themselves from the strictures of drive theory. Most of the early writers emphasized the importance of primary relationships, particularly the mother–child relationship (Fairbairn, 1959/1962; Guntrip, 1973; Klein & Riviere, 1953; Winnicott, 1997), but these theorists, possibly out of loyalty to Freud, still carried forward both instinct models and drive language. Melanie Klein (Klein & Riviere, 1953), perhaps the grandmother of American object relations theory, believed that the capacity for concern grows out of guilt over injuries inflicted on the caregiver. Winnicott (1997) is known for his lyrical descriptions of the mother–infant dyad, but he saw guilt about aggression at the core of the growth of the capacity for concern. Fairbairn and Guntrip stepped a bit farther away from Freudian drive theory with their emphasis on mature dependence (Fairbairn, 1959/1962) and mutuality (Guntrip, 1973). Still, object relations theorists were bound to a world of relationships based on primary drives aimed at satisfying objects, a vision fundamentally different from RCT, which posits a primary motivation toward engaging in relationship.

Daniel Stern's close observations of mother–infant interactions led him to grasp the basic mutuality between mother and child, and he struggled to move away from Freudian drive language (Stern, 1986). He also documented mutual regulation between mother and infant, thus helping us see that from the outset, there is mutual change and growth in the mother–infant interaction. The infant is not a tabula rasa, and development is not a one-way street. This represented an important movement away from the more traditional psychoanalytic theories. In the field of psychoanalysis, the theorists known as relational psychoanalysts (Mitchell, 1988) began to use the notion of a two-person psychology in clinical practice. Others developed ideas about mutuality (Aron, 1996) and intersubjectivity (Stolorow & Atwood, 1992) that have much in common with the RCT model. However, these relational psychoanalysts and intersubjective theorists continue to view resolution of unconscious conflict via interpretation as the primary task of therapy. Although RCT honors the importance of meaning making in therapy, it sees the task of therapy as facilitating fuller movement into relationship (Winnicott, 1963).

Even as therapeutic models became increasingly relational, they maintained the primacy of the individuated self. Kohut's self-psychology (1984) is often viewed as a primarily relational approach. But it is important to remember that, for Kohut, the goal of both development and therapy was supporting the growth of a cohesive self. The name of his work—*self psychology*—accurately reflects the biases in his model. Early on, Kohut posited that in the best of all possible worlds, one outgrows one's need for "selfobjects" to regulate self-cohesion and self-esteem. The more a person can internalize self-esteem regulation and cohesiveness, the better. However, late in life, Kohut recognized that, in the real world, we all need "selfobjects" throughout our lives. We depend on others to help us create meaning, feel intact, and maintain healthy self-worth. Nevertheless, in Kohut's "ideal" world, all of these functions would be internalized in the form of intrapsychic structure. Again, the bias is against depending on others. The need to depend on others for self-object function is seen as a sign of lack of mature development. Kohut's model, although it beautifully explores empathy and the way we "know" one another's experience, is also not a model of mutual growth. In the parent–child relationship, the emphasis is on the functions the parent provides for the baby; in the therapy relationship, the emphasis is on one-way empathy, from therapist to client. There is no indication of what we call *mutual empathy*, which is a cornerstone of RCT.

Carl Rogers moved away from the psychoanalytic model in his creation of client-centered therapy. He stressed authenticity, accurate empathy, and warmth (Rogers, 1951), all of which are important in RCT as well. Interestingly, the followers of Rogers have tended to emphasize his technique, sometimes overlooking his broader philosophical understanding of therapy and change. In his later years, Rogers noted that he felt his very being, his presence, was of great importance in the healing process. Yet even then, Rogers did not take the next step RCT takes, which is to locate the healing in the therapeutic relationship itself. RCT might be characterized as "relationship-centered therapy" in contrast with Rogers's client-centered therapy.

RCT departs from these mainstream theories by naming the biases represented in their theories of self and clearly stating the primacy of relationship in people's lives. It emphasizes the development of mutuality and factors in the effects of power dynamics on all relationships and thus on all mental health and societal well-being. Rather than celebrating the bounded individual, it posits that chronic disconnection is the source of enormous suffering and that healing people's experience of isolation is one of the central tasks of psychotherapy.

CRITICAL RESPONSES TO RCT

The initial reception of RCT was mixed. Many therapists, mostly women, found resonance in the theory being expounded at the Stone Center. Just as Miller's (1976) *Toward a New Psychology of Women* had been a surprise bestseller in the late 1970s and early 1980s, in the 1990s, *Women's Growth in Connection* (Jordan et al., 1991) quickly became a classic in women's studies and clinical programs. Many women spoke of Miller's book as "changing their lives." In response to *Women's Growth in Connection* and an article in the *Boston Globe* magazine featuring the work of the original theory group (Robb, 1988), therapists made comments such as, "This is the way I do therapy but I never thought it was okay. I thought I wasn't being authoritative or neutral enough ... but I knew being connected and responsive was working. I just didn't have any theory to back up what I believed."

However, others, particularly those from more traditional analytic schools of thought, were openly troubled and nervous that RCT would lead to the loss of therapeutic neutrality. Many suggested the model was "dangerous" because it invited more engagement on the part of the therapist. They were particularly worried that "boundaries" would become lax and therapists and clients could more easily be violated (Miller & Stiver, 1997; Robb, 2006). Some felt anxious that the emphasis on therapist authenticity would lead to boundary violations and inappropriate self-disclosure on the part of therapists. The language of mutual empathy was misinterpreted as suggesting total equality and sameness of role; some suggested it would lead to clients' feeling called upon to take care of their therapists.

The fears about therapist authenticity and responsiveness failed to take into account several factors that were explicitly noted by relational–cultural theorists. The therapeutic relationship in RCT is not an ordinary social relationship. There are therapeutic roles (therapist and client) that carry different expectations and responsibilities. There are also ethical and legal considerations that guide the work. The therapist holds responsibility for the well-being of the client (to the extent that is possible). Therapy is always guided by attention to what contributes to the client's well-being or healing. Therapeutic authenticity in no way means total spontaneity; it involves finding, in the therapeutic interaction, the emotional truth that can be used to assist the client's healing. It depends on therapist responsiveness, coupled with being aware of the possible impact on the other person and caring about that impact (wanting it to be positive and growth producing). The therapist's responsiveness, emotional engagement, and authenticity are nuanced, complicated, and necessary for healing. New therapists need to be carefully supervised in developing the capacity to participate in this kind of interaction.

RCT's reevaluation of the concept of boundaries stimulated apprehension in some therapists. There was concern that without the traditional focus on firm, strong boundaries, RCT would somehow contribute to increased abuse and violation of clients. Critics failed to appreciate RCT's reframing of what boundaries mean (Jordan, 1995a), however. The traditional therapeutic emphasis on boundaries arose within the separate self paradigm, which stresses the importance of protecting the organism from an impinging environment. In that model, boundaries keep dangerous stimuli out and provide structure and containment for internal structures and processes—hence, the emphasis on the therapist maintaining "strict boundaries" for the protection of the client. Rather than invoking the more abstract concept of boundaries per se, RCT explicitly delineates expectations for therapists around issues like safety, clarity, and the capacity to say no. By overtly addressing the therapist's responsibility for the client's well-being and supporting the therapist in upholding that responsibility, RCT creates a space where therapist and client can safely address relationship issues without stumbling over what are commonly called *boundary issues.* Indeed, because this term is usually applied within a separate self model, RCT proposes looking critically at the issues that are covered by the boundary concept.

Those concerned about neutrality and boundaries were not the only critics of RCT. Christina Robb (2006) noted, "In the course of changing many ways our society works, relational psychology has been demonized, trivialized and mythologized" (p. xx). Some theorists dismissed the model because of its feminist roots, arguing that it was thus of little import or flawed by a "warm and fuzzy" message (Aron, 1996). Sommers (1994) attacked the emphasis it put on the sociopolitical implications of gender. Some felt it was too simplistic and not sufficiently appreciative of the complexity of healing in therapy. Others looked askance at the whole field of clinical qualitative research and considered RCT an unsubstantiated theory (Sharf, 2008). Each of these critiques reveals how RCT threatened some of the fundamental assumptions of mainstream therapeutic practices.

FEMINIST RESPONSES TO RCT

RCT and feminist approaches have much in common, but although many feminists embraced the work (Belenky, Clinchy, Goldberger, & Tarule, 1986; L. M. Brown & Gilligan, 1992; Gilligan, Lyons, & Hanmer, 1990;

Jack, 1999; Lerner, 1985; Pipher, 1994), others were more critical (Brown & Ballou, 2002). A persistent refrain was that RCT was "essentialist," stuck in a portrayal of essential differences between men and women (Barnett & Rivers, 2004). Behind this critique lay the fear that RCT would be used to push women back into traditional, diminished roles. A theory that valorizes women's relational skills was deemed a threat to women who were attempting to break out of traditional caregiving roles (Walsh, 1997; Westkott, 1997). Barnett and Rivers (2004), two feminist critics of relational psychology, specifically warned that relational theory can be misused to keep women in a "down" position. Their solution was to throw out the theory rather than continue to draw attention to the ways any theory can be co-opted to support the position of a dominant group.

There was also uneasiness with the idea that RCT encouraged self-sacrifice and altruism. In fact, RCT attempts to move away from the dichotomies of selfish versus selfless or self versus other and toward an account of growth that encompasses mutual growth. Others cautioned that RCT did not adequately appreciate the power of social construction in creating gender straitjackets. Westkott (1997) argued that the relational theory of women's development perpetuates male privilege. On the other hand, K. Johnson and Ferguson (1990), authors of a guidebook on the psychology of women, noted that RCT comes "closest to creating a comprehensive pro-female psychological theory that rivals Freud's pro-male perspective" (p. 36).

The essentialist criticism has always been puzzling. From its start, RCT has been solidly anchored in social constructivist thinking. *Toward a New Psychology of Women*, Miller's foundational work of 1976, is largely based on an analysis of the social construction of gender and the significance of power relationships in creating limiting images and expectations for women. By making power dynamics so central to its understanding of human development, RCT has explicitly noted the importance of context in shaping us, collectively and individually. RCT has often viewed gender, the part that emphasizes difference, as formed by stereotypes, power dynamics, and sex-role standards that are imposed in child development. In fact, the only essentialist position that RCT holds is its belief that we all grow through and toward relationship throughout the life span. As Robb (2006) wrote, "Relational psychologists are saying not that women are essentially nurturant but that nurturant human connection is essential" (p. xxiii).

RCT AND ADVANCES IN BRAIN SCIENCE

In recent years, RCT has begun to pay attention to the profound effects of brain structure, neurochemistry, and hormone differences on psychological development. This includes appreciation of differential shaping of male and female brains. The current use of functional magnetic resonance imaging and the study of brain structure and functioning support many of RCT's early insights about the fundamental relationality of human beings. Recent findings from the world of neuroscience suggest that human beings are "hardwired to connect"—that we come into the world primed to connect and to find responsiveness (Banks, 2011, 2016). We also arrive primed to be responsive, to engage with others. Our survival depends on finding a responsive other person, not just to provide physical nourishment but to engage with us and stimulate our emotional and neurological growth. Thus, babies who are not responded to languish and even die. Eisenberger and Lieberman (2004) suggested that relational connection is as fundamental for human life as air, water, and food. In their social pain overlap theory (SPOT), they delineated the way that social pain and physical pain travel the same pathways to the same place in the brain (the anterior cingulate cortex): Social pain and physical pain are indistinguishable. Pain is pain. The conclusion drawn from this research is that connections are so essential to our lives that we are neurologically "wired" to respond to exclusion and isolation in the same way that we respond to physical pain, lack of air and water, or other life-threatening events. Without connection, we are endangered. An alarm sounds when we are isolated or excluded or when we even anticipate being without connection. Our brains grow in relationship, and neurons die when we do not find connection (Chugani et al., 2001). Relationships aren't simply "feel good" experiences; they are at the core of our human survival (Banks,

2016; Lieberman, 2013). In mutual interaction, whether between baby and mother, between friend and friend, or between therapist and client, both brains change (Schore, 1994; Siegel, 1999). When we are deprived of healthy connection, we suffer.

The discovery of mirror neurons (Iacoboni, 2009) and the "smart vagus" (Porges, 2011) supports the contention that we are hardwired for empathic responsiveness and connection: "Mirror neurons make emotions contagious, letting the feelings we witness flow through us, helping us get in synch and follow what's going on" (Goleman, 2006, p. 42). In other words, to understand the other, we resonate with one another. In these interactions, both people are changed. These neurons fire when watching the actions or emotions of others; for example, when watching someone else be pricked by a pin, a corresponding pain center is activated in the observer (Hoffman, 1978; Hutchison, Davis, Lozano, Tasker, & Dostrovsky, 1999). Mirror neurons provide an underpinning for the development of full empathy and support the theory of a hardwired capacity for resonance with others. Empathy is the experiential anchor of our essential human connectivity. Empathy is profoundly important to our sense of relatedness, belonging, and meaning and can be defined as a deep sense of both being understood and understanding. Empathy is not an either–or, reciprocal process but a mutual joining and "feeling-knowing with." Mirror neurons contribute to empathy, which in turn contributes to concern for others and the capacity to learn from one's impact on others; empathy helps build communities where differences are honored and vulnerability is supported. Mutual empathy can provide the foundation for healthy and thriving individuals and generate deeply caring communities.

The most recent brain research emphasizes the power of neuro-plasticity (Begley, 2008; Cozolino, 2014; Doidge, 2007; Schore, 1994). RCT posits that the most significant changes and personal growth originate in relationships. It has now been shown that relationships change brains (Cozolino, 2014; Goleman, 2006; Schore, 1994; Siegel, 1999). While hurtful and abusive relationships shape the brain in such a way that the orbitofrontal cortex fails to function effectively to create adaptive social functioning, positive relationships such as therapy can rework these earlier pathways (Banks, 2016; Schore, 1994; Siegel, 1999). Schore (1994) noted that

> our interactions play a role in re-shaping our brain, through neuroplasticity—the ways repeated experiences sculpt the shape, size and number of neurons and their synaptic connections. Some potent shaping occurs in our key relationships by repeatedly driving our brain into a given register. (as quoted in Goleman, 2006, p. 171; see also Banks, 2016; Frederickson, 2013)

Rather than seeing the new information from neuroscience as contributing to a deterministic understanding of relationships, we find tremendous hope in the new data on brain plasticity. Brains can change and grow. And we believe that connections with people are crucial to most brain change. Davidson, who has demonstrated that with mental training, humans can change our own emotional brain patterns, noted:

> We have far more control over our wellbeing, over how we respond to the world, than simplistic, deterministic views would permit. This work leaves us with a much more hopeful and optimistic message. It also places more responsibility on us. (as quoted in Bures, 2007)

SUMMARY

RCT is, by some standards, a relative newcomer to the psychological community. When its originators first started thinking and writing about connection and disconnection in the late 1970s, the work was quite controversial. More than 40 years later, many of these ideas have come to be seen as mainstream, and some are thoroughly assimilated into other approaches. Others have come to similar insights without being aware of the work of RCT. It is likely that early on, RCT became marginalized as a theory because it was seen as a theory "only" by and about women (e.g., Aron, 1996). In fact, it is a clinical and developmental model based on a compelling revision of human development from the point of view of the centrality of relationship in people's lives. What still marks RCT as special, different, and even perhaps revolutionary is its integration and appreciation of the centrality of relationship, the pain of isolation, the importance of power stratifications in creating disconnections and significant distress, and the ways in which our brains are programmed for connection. RCT points to the inherent dilemma for people living in a culture of disconnection: Our brains and bodies are meant to grow in connection, but the messages of our culture are that we should be independent and self-sufficient. We are born to connect but taught to stand on our own two feet. Our culture pits our neurobiology, which seeks connection, against our cultural prescriptions, which advocate independence and separation. This clash creates significant stress for individuals as they strive to attain unrealizable states of autonomy and independence, all the while needing connection. We are invited to deny or ignore our need for human connection. Furthermore, needing others is often pathologized (e.g., "the dependent personality"). We misperceive self-interest as being a biological imperative rather than see it for what it is: a social prescription that can be altered by shifting cultural values and socialization practices.

3

Theory

Relational–cultural theory (RCT) arose from an effort to better understand the importance of growth-fostering relationships in people's lives. It seeks to lessen the suffering caused by chronic disconnection and isolation, whether at an individual or societal level, to increase the capacity for relational resilience, and to foster social justice. M. Walker (2002b) described how the connections and disconnections that characterize relationships occur in a context that has been "raced, engendered, sexualized and stratified along dimensions of class, physical ability, religion or whatever constructions carry ontological significance in the culture" (p. 2). The effects of privilege, marginalization, and cultural forces are seen by RCT as central to psychological development (Jordan & Hartling, 2002). Relational–cultural theorists have "depicted culture as more than the scenic backdrop for the unfolding of development; rather, culture is viewed as an active agent in relational processes that shape human possibility"

http://dx.doi.org/10.1037/0000063-003
Relational–Cultural Therapy, Second Edition, by J. V. Jordan
Copyright © 2018 by the American Psychological Association. All rights reserved.

(M. Walker, 2005, p. 48). The insight that relational development is always completely suffused with social and cultural identities has been central to the development and practice of RCT. Further, these social and cultural identities are stratified and accorded differing amounts of social respect and power. They often become sources of chronic disconnection and disempowerment.

Although the RCT model was originally developed to better represent women's experiences, it has become clear that men's psychological growth has also been distorted by the lenses used to study it (Levant & Powell, 2017). Men's desires and needs for connection have been denied and made invisible. The dominant culture has demanded that men achieve the goals of independence, autonomy, and individualistic competitive achievement. The denial of vulnerability, the need for a strong and separate self, and the reliance on power over others as the path to safety has exacted enormous costs for men (Pollack, 1998). William Pollack (1998) wrote about what he called the normative trauma of male socialization, and Ron Levant (1992) outlined what he called normative alexithymia in men schooled in a "strong," stiff-upper-lip, tough, hard, nonfeminine masculinity. The dominant culture has also created particular pressure on mothers to push their sons toward separation; mothers are blamed for tying their sons to their apron strings or feminizing them by investing in close and caring relationships with them (Lombardi, 2011). Today, RCT hopes to better represent both women's and men's psychological experience as it seeks transformation of chronic disconnection into connection and empowerment for individuals of both genders and for society as a whole.

CORE CONCEPTS

The core concepts of RCT (Jordan, 2000) include the following:

1. People grow through and toward relationship throughout the lifespan.
2. Movement toward mutuality rather than separation characterizes mature functioning.
3. Relationship differentiation and elaboration characterize growth.

4. Mutual empathy and mutual empowerment are at the core of growth-fostering relationships.
5. Authenticity is necessary for real engagement and full participation in growth-fostering relationships.
6. In growth-fostering relationships, all people contribute and grow or benefit. Development is not a one-way street.
7. One of the goals of development from a relational perspective is the development of increased relational competence and capacities over the lifespan.
8. Mutual empathy is the primary means through which we grow. Placing mutual empathy at the core of human development not only affects the individual but also contributes to the growth of a just society. Social justice is the outcome of the practice of mutuality in which the needs and experience of both people in any given interaction are respected and honored.

Authenticity

The ability to represent oneself as fully as possible in relationship and be responded to with empathy contributes to mutual growth and well-being. Authenticity, however, must be informed by anticipatory empathy for it to serve a positive relational outcome. Thus, we are not suggesting a kind of amygdala authenticity in which a person, without thinking about their impact on the other person ("being real"), blurts out any passing thought or feeling. Relational authenticity exists to serve relationship. When we look at it from this vantage it must be informed by anticipation of the possible impact on the other person (anticipatory empathy). Total honesty without regard for how we affect others is neither desirable nor useful. We find the "one true thing" we can offer, not every random association we might have. Our intention, particularly in therapy, is that this authenticity will promote healing and growth. Responsiveness depends on emotional attunement but also on active executive functioning. We have complex brains that, at their best, work in an integrated manner to create balance and flexibility, contributing to effective social interaction and relational well-being and resilience (Banks, 2016; Porges, 2011; Siegel, 1999).

Mutual Empathy and Growth-Fostering Relationships

In sum, rather than moving toward greater separateness and independence, the goal is to increase our capacity for relational resilience, mutual empathy, and mutual empowerment. Mutual empathy is the core process that allows for growth in relationship. In a dyad, it involves the responsiveness of two people, but it can occur between more people as well. In this movement of empathy, with each person affected by and seeing her impact on the other, the individual sees the possibility for change and connection. Thus, aspects of one's experience that have been split off and seen as unacceptable or threatening begin to come back into relationship. When protective strategies of disconnection are operating, people remain stuck in old patterns of disconnection. Under these conditions, there is not much room for growth. In mutual empathy, people begin to see that they can bring more and more of themselves into relationship. In this process, they become more present, more open to change and learning.

The need for connection in which growth is a priority is the core motivation in people's lives. In growth-fostering relationships, people are able to bring themselves most fully and authentically into connection. Jean Baker Miller suggested that these relationships have five outcomes ("the five good things"): a sense of zest; a better understanding of self, other, and the relationship (clarity); a sense of worth; an enhanced capacity to act or be productive; and an increased desire for more connection (Miller & Stiver, 1997).

Disconnection

RCT sees disconnections as normative and inevitable in relationships; they occur when one person misunderstands, invalidates, excludes, humiliates, or injures the other person in some way. Acute disconnections occur frequently in all relationships. If they can be addressed and reworked, they are not problematic; in fact, they become places of enormous growth. When an injured person, particularly one who has less power, can represent her or his experience of disconnection or pain to the more powerful person and be responded to, with interest or concern, the less powerful, hurt person has a sense of "mattering," of having an effect on the other. This strengthens connection as well as a sense of relational competence. Thus, places of empathic failure can become places of increasing trust and strength in relationships.

If, however, the less powerful person is not allowed or encouraged to voice her or his hurt or anger, that person will learn to suppress that aspect of her or his experience. She or he learns to move into hiding and inauthenticity to stay in relationship. Often with shame or withdrawal, the person moves out of genuine, growth-producing relationship. Furthermore, the person twists herself or himself to fit in, to be acceptable to this powerful other person. The person feels profoundly disempowered and unseen. The relationship itself is diminished by these exchanges, and if they occur repeatedly, a condition of chronic disconnection develops. In this situation, the less powerful, injured person feels she or he is to blame for the disconnection and feels immobilized and increasingly isolated. The injured person brings less and less of her or his real experience into the relationship and often loses touch with her or his own feelings and inner experience. Although this dynamic creates isolation and disempowerment at the personal level, it also preserves the politics of dominance. In this way, the personal is political, the political is personal, and the rewriting of a psychological paradigm becomes an act of social justice.

Relational Images

Relational images are the inner constructions and expectations we each create out of our experience in relationships (Miller & Stiver, 1997). They develop early in life and are carried from one relationship to another, sometimes subject to modification (growth) and sometimes limiting our expectations in ways that anchor us in the relational past. Our expectations of relationships are held in these relational images. These images are also shaped by societal forces and values; devaluation of marginalized groups leads to disconnection and negative expectations for oneself and one's relationships. These images affect one's sense of worth and participation in the larger community. Chronic disconnections lead to negative relational images. When relational images are flexible, they can be modified and do not generate inappropriate generalizations. However, when they are rigidified and overly generalized, they keep us from participating fully in the actual relationship at hand. In this way, they operate similarly to what many psychodynamic models refer to as transference in therapy, bringing expectations from the past to bear on the present in a way that distorts current reality.

Freud (1912/1958) believed that therapist neutrality and objectivity were necessary for transference to develop; in contrast, RCT sees "transference" phenomena emerging in all relationships. In this context, "replication becomes problematic when it keeps people 'stuck in the past' and not free to engage in new relationships in the present" (Miller & Stiver, 1997, p. 138). RCT further suggests that "neutrality" and distance on the part of the therapist can interfere with moving into a new and different relational experience in therapy. With therapeutic authenticity and responsiveness, the therapist can actively participate in helping to reshape relational images:

> Memories of one's past relationships, with their history of connections and disconnections, shape the content and complexities of the relational images people bring into therapy. These images inform the expectations people have about relationships in general, but in therapy they become the focus of exploration. (Miller & Stiver, 1997, p. 139)

Alteration of relational images leads to personal growth. Understanding and naming the cultural dynamics that create marginalization and denigration lead to empowerment and the possibility of participating in social change as well as personal growth.

In therapy, the therapist and client also search for exceptions to the dominant relational images; these are known as *discrepant relational images.* If a core relational image is, "Whenever I make my needs known, I will be abandoned," a discrepant relational image might be, "My Aunt Cathy was really there for me whenever I needed her. She liked my spunkiness." The negative relational image "When I get angry at people, they retaliate by rejecting me" could be contradicted by the discrepant relational image "My brother used to stick with me and validate my anger." If negative relational images contribute to a sense of hopelessness and isolation, these discrepant relational images challenge their "pathological certainty"; they are places of hope and relational possibility on which therapists can help expand.

Often, profound reworking of these negative relational images occurs around empathic failures in the therapy relationship itself. If one assumes that negative relational images and a sense of woundedness and self-blame arose in situations where the individual was unable to represent the pain of her experience to the other more powerful person, being able to represent the pain of being misunderstood or not seen by the therapist to the therapist and having that representation acknowledged and addressed can open previously closed doors. The repair of these disconnections is at the heart of therapy. In these repairs, the individual's sense of insignificance, relational incompetence, and isolation shifts. Relational expectations and neurological circuits are modified as the therapist responds to the client in ways that disconfirm the entrenched and limiting relational images. Negative relational images begin to change, relational expectations are altered, and the effects of shame and self-blame give way to self-empathy and hope. These transformations, although sometimes incremental, are profound, and they bring the client into current reality with the ability to develop current relationships. This condition has been referred to as *relational mindfulness* (Surrey, 2005; Surrey & Eldridge, 2007) or *relational awareness* (Jordan, 1995b).

Jean Baker Miller (1989) developed the notion of *condemned isolation* to capture the fixedness and pain of the relational images that keep us locked out of relationship and therefore out of hope. In condemned isolation we feel immobilized, unworthy, and alone, and we feel that we have created this reality. The individual feels that she or he is to blame for her or his powerlessness and hopelessness and that there is something intrinsically "wrong" with her or him. Under such conditions, she or he will not risk the vulnerability necessary to make connections. The threat of further isolation is simply too great. Miller and Stiver (1997) coined the term *central relational paradox* to capture what happens in this situation. Although we deeply desire and need connections, we are terrified of what will happen if we move into the vulnerability necessary to make deep connection, so we keep large aspects of ourselves out of connection. We develop strategies of disconnection, trying to protect ourselves by disconnecting, keeping parts of ourselves split off. We develop these strategies to avoid isolation, but paradoxically, they contribute to our sense of isolation and being unseen. In her research with adolescent girls, Gilligan (1990) formulated an almost identical paradox. She documented the ways in which girls in early adolescence seem to lose certain outspoken and insightful parts of themselves as they attempt to fit into the kinds of relationships the culture prescribes for them. The extreme of this dissociation from one's own inner experience occurs in sexual and physical abuse (Herman, 1992). We thus see how these strategies and their consequences can result from social forces, as well as from individual experiences (Banks, 2016).

Controlling Images and Shame

Controlling images also create patterns of isolation and disempowerment. African American sociologist Patricia Hill Collins (1990, 2000) has explored the ways society creates controlling images to shame and disempower certain groups. They define who we are, what is acceptable, and what we can do. Collins (2000) noted that controlling images—such as stereotypes of "mammies, matriarchs, welfare mothers"—are actually lies that hold people in their "place" and induce the notion that change cannot happen. These defining images feel real and immutable. It is hard for people to stay with their own truth when they are immersed in a sea of distorting and controlling images. Often, these societal controlling images become part of an individual's relational images: "From a Relational-Cultural perspective, strategies of disconnection give rise to internalized oppression, a complex of relational images grounded in the distortions and disinformation required to normalize the inequalities of a power-over culture" (M. Walker, 2005, p. 54).

Strategies of disconnection frequently arise around shame and a sense of unworthiness. Shame is a contributing factor to much immobilization and a major source of chronic disconnection:

> In shame, one feels disconnected, that one's being is at fault, that one
> is unworthy of empathic response, or that one is unlovable. Often in
> shame people move out of connection, lose their sense of efficacy and
> lose their ability to authentically represent their experience. (Jordan,
> 2000, p. 1008)

Shame arises naturally when people feel that their "being" is unworthy, that if people knew them more fully, they would reject or scorn them (Hartling, Rosen, Walker, & Jordan, 2000). Tomkins (1987) considered shame one of the original affects, present from birth and reflected in gaze aversion. Shame is also imposed on people, however, to control and disempower them.

Shaming is a powerful way to silence and isolate individuals, but it also plays a large role in silencing and disempowering marginalized groups whose members are strategically, if often invisibly, shamed to reinforce their isolation and thus their subordination: "Isolation is the glue that holds oppression in place" (Laing, 1998). A dominant group's authority can be maintained by the widespread power tactic of silencing those who present differing views of reality. Microaggressions, in which seemingly small acts of violence or disrespect go unnamed and unchallenged, are a part of the invisibility of these power tactics (Jenkins, 1993). In particular, when the dominant group inevitably and strategically discourages open conflict and expression of difference by the nondominant groups, differences are framed as signs of deficiency. The marginalized groups often internalize the dominant group's standards, and internalized oppression (Lipsky, 1987) functions to perpetuate the shame and disempowerment.

Often, moving from group shame to a sense of worth is based on the effects of creating cohesive group pride (gay pride, Black pride, girl power, Black Lives Matter). Creating or joining a community buffers individuals from the disempowerment of marginalization. In these collective, empowering movements out of shame, people reclaim their dignity and their right to be respected by others. In *The Skin We're In*, Janie Ward (2000) wrote about the importance to Black adolescent girls of actively creating healthy resistance (liberation resistance) to the dominant White norms that threaten to silence and isolate them. She pointed to the importance of thinking critically about the dominant realities, naming them, and opposing them with alternative versions of reality. This creates a sense of positive identity and undermines the notion of *THE reality* or *THE truth*, which often is only a panoply of "controlling images" (Collins, 2000; Robinson & Ward, 1991; J. V. Ward, 2000). Since Janie Ward's contribution, other authors, including Ta-Nehisi Coates (2015) and Jesmyn Ward (2016), have amplified modern aspects of race and identity.

It is essential that clinicians recognize the multiple sources of shame that bring people into therapy. Helen Block Lewis coded transcripts of hundreds of psychotherapy sessions and found that shame was by far the most common emotion patients expressed (Lewis, 1987). RCT's focus on helping individuals build and rebuild their capacity for growth-fostering relationships calls for taking into account any and all forces affecting that capacity, including, especially, oppressive social systems. Racial identity models (Helms & Cook, 1999) allow us to understand how deeply racial/ethnic identity issues are woven into our social fabric and how profoundly they affect relational possibilities. Controlling images and shame have a profound impact on development: "How one is regarded by the culture influences one's ability to negotiate developmental tasks" (M. Walker, 2005, p. 50). Neuroscience now shows us undeniably that social exclusion hurts us; being left out, shamed, and treated as "devalued other" creates real pain and injury (Lieberman, 2013). This is true at the individual and the social levels. Therapists and clients can work together to understand and address the effect of controlling images, shame, and oppression: "Given the foundational premise [of RCT] that healthy development occurs through action-in-relationship, it follows that developmental potential is enhanced when an individual can function free of the inhibiting objectifications that limit the range of growth and possibility" (M. Walker, 2005, p. 50). We empower others so that they in turn can empower others. Mutual growth occurs. Under these conditions, social justice becomes a reality, and social change unfolds. The dynamics of shame and oppression can also pertain to dyadic relationships, particularly abuse situations, in which the perpetrator often shames and isolates the target.

The *central relational paradox* suggests that when a person has been humiliated, hurt, or violated in early relationships, the yearning for connection actually increases. Yet at the same time, the person develops an exaggerated sense that the vulnerability necessary to enter authentic relationship is not safe. Thus, there is an enhanced desire for connection and an increased fear of seeking connection. In therapy it becomes important for the therapist to honor this central relational paradox. The therapist must be respectful of the strategies of disconnection and must deeply understand why they were developed and how they helped keep the person alive at crucial times in unresponsive or violating relationships. The therapist must "feel with" the client in the sense of really "getting it," developing a contextual empathy that helps her or him see the conditions that created this need for self-protection through disconnection. At the same time, the therapist must hold the overarching, even if tentatively embraced, desire for more real connection. In moving from chronic disconnection to connection, supported by the therapist, the client will begin to relinquish strategies of disconnection and, in so doing, will have to experience a certain sense of vulnerability and risk. As the client begins to relinquish the strategies of disconnection, the therapist will need to expect sudden disconnects after increased closeness or authenticity, when the client reverts to old patterns of safety. The therapist does not push for more connection at these times but honors both the yearning for connection and the need to disconnect to feel safe. In part, the work of therapy involves differentiating current relational possibilities from old relational images. It involves introducing uncertainty into the client's overly generalized and fixed negative relational images (e.g., shifting "When I show my tenderness, I get beaten up" to "When I was vulnerable as a child my stepfather beat me, but my current boyfriend is there for me.") and helping the client experience new relationships for him- or herself.

Relational Resilience and Relational Courage

RCT suggests that developing *relational resilience*—the capacity to move back into connection after disconnection and the capacity to reach out for help—is crucial to anyone's healing. It also explicitly states that resilience and courage are not traits that a person has or does not have; these characteristics are built in relationship, and they wither when growth-fostering relationships are not available (Hartling, 2005; Jordan, 2013). Therapists must be careful not to force or push connection with clients, however. Instead, we should slowly, deliberately provide experiences of safe connection and of reworking empathic failures. Therapists must demonstrate to clients that the well-being of the relationship and the client is more important than certainty, being right, or maintaining our own self-images as "good, empathic therapists." Thus, we work actively with disconnections and relational failures. We apologize when we are wrong. We work with our own defensiveness when under attack, not assuming automatically that the entire problem is in the client (e.g., not turning to "projective identification" to explain our own reactions in therapy). We are open to examining our own limitations, as well as the ways our own disconnections injure or affect others. Working with mutual empathy, the therapist allows clients to see their impact on her or him—that they matter to her or him. The therapist realizes that relational information is important for clients who need to see how they affect others and, in some cases, rework the ways they express themselves so that they can effectively create positive results through the effect they have on others. As therapists, we are not Delphic oracles, providing mythic interpretations, unlocking obscure conflicts, or seeing with total clarity beyond the clouded and limited vision of our clients. Instead, we are engaged in healing connections that challenge us as therapists to bring awareness and openness to the process of therapy. We are often participating in an ongoing process of connection and disconnection and working to shed some light on the flow of relationship.

Related to the concept of relational resilience is *relational courage*. This concept challenges the usual sense of courage as an internal trait, characteristic of individuals who undertake enormous risks alone (e.g., scaling sheer cliffs or parachuting out of airplanes). The traditional notion of courage carries the expectation that strong people will not experience fear or uncertainty in frightening situations. This undoubtedly contributes to the overemphasis on risk-taking and defiance of fear in popular portrayals of manhood. An RCT understanding of courage suggests that courage involves feeling the fear and finding support to deal with it. Thus, RCT talks about the importance of en-*couraging* other people: helping develop courage in one another. Encouragement is akin to empowerment; it involves facilitating the development and maintenance of a sense of confidence and hope in the face of trying conditions.

RCT contributes to a cohesive approach to doing psychotherapy, but it also serves as a conceptual framework for undertaking social action. RCT practitioners in clinical settings frame their work around healing the suffering of the individuals they see in treatment. But they also recognize a larger mission of changing the social conditions that create much of the suffering that people endure. RCT work is not about changing people to fit into dysfunctional cultural conditions but empowering them to heal in connection and in turn to heal others in connection. A part of the ripple effect of growth in connection often spills into participating in social change by creating alliances or communities that are built around relational values. RCT can be seen as a means to bridge relational, multicultural, and social justice competencies (Comstock et al., 2008).

4

The Therapy Process

In clinical practice, relational–cultural therapists are guided by our desires to lessen the experience of isolation, increase the capacity for self-empathy and empathy for others, and develop an appreciation of the power of context and limiting cultural/relational images. Relational–cultural theory (RCT) therapy depends more on an attitude and quality of mutual engagement than on any specific techniques or interventions. RCT therapy offers clients radical respect and a deep appreciation of their suffering and of the ways they have learned to survive when important relationships have been hurtful. It views isolation and chronic disconnection as the cause of much of the suffering that brings clients into treatment. RCT therapy seeks to lessen the experience of condemned isolation in the therapy relationship in order to help clients transform their lives outside therapy. To achieve this goal, the therapist attends carefully to the flow of connections and disconnections, both in clients' lives and in the therapy relationship.

http://dx.doi.org/10.1037/0000063-004
Relational–Cultural Therapy, Second Edition, by J. V. Jordan

The movement of mutual empathy creates necessary safety and provides important information that allows clients to begin to move from protective disconnection back into growth-fostering connection.

ASSESSMENT PHASE

In the assessment of clients, RCT therapy gathers information on the usual demographics: age, education, living arrangements, economic/class background, ethnicity, work, and other interests. It pays particular attention to significant relationships, past and present, and seeks early on to understand clients' purpose and goals for seeking assistance. In addition to examining the pain that brings people into treatment, RCT therapy looks for strengths and coping skills that clients have developed, including how effective these coping skills are and what degree of empathy clients exhibit with their own experience (self-empathy) and with others. RCT therapy places a special emphasis on assessing resilience—in particular, relational resilience—including what support systems clients participate in (both those where they receive support and those where they provide it to others), whether they have a sense of "belonging" or "mattering" somewhere in their lives, and how authentic they can be in their primary relationships. Personal and societal sources of disempowerment are also taken into account. Is the person part of a marginalized group? Is there support within that group? Has the person been a target of either microaggressions or more blatant discrimination and social exclusion? Has the person been subjected to personal or societal trauma?

Another important area to explore is the client's ability to engage in constructive conflict. This can be a particularly useful area for uncovering the client's relational images. The therapist considers whether the client can represent her or his needs and views to others when they conflict with the other person's stance. If not, is this because of real limitations in the current relationship or limiting relational images? An assessment should evaluate the relational images that the client brings to therapy, beginning with the dominant, core relational images that often transfer widely to other relationships. These relational images can be thought of as relational expectations that guide the person's current interpersonal engagements. These expectations may be conveyed in an if–then statement as in "If I am (fill in the blank), then the other person will (fill in the blank)." For example, "If I need something from someone, they treat me badly." In addition to trying to develop a working model of these relational images, the therapist pays attention to how overly generalized these images are to current relationships and how much certainty is attached to the expectations. The therapist attempts to determine whether current relationships actually replicate earlier relationships or whether they in fact offer other possibilities for growth. Discrepant relational images are also noted; these are the images that challenge the "pathological certainty" of the negative images and often become pivotal to hope and change.

Another focus of assessment is the person's strategies of disconnection—that is, what methods are used to disengage from others? The first questions are about the origin of these strategies: Where were they learned? For what purpose? How effective were they? The next step is to attempt to develop some perspective on how useful these strategies are currently. Although context makes a significant difference in terms of the possibility of reconnecting after disconnections, it is important to get a picture of the individual's capacity for reconnection, including the ease of asking for help and showing vulnerability and self-awareness. Attunement to possible trauma and a history of relational violations helps the therapist assess the possible degree of chronic disconnection and protective inauthenticity. The therapist also listens for possible sources of shame, although these are rarely examined directly in the assessment phase. In attending to relational patterns, a person's history of loss and grief is also of interest. Where have relationships led to hope and a sense of possibility, and where have they ended in grief or deep disappointment?

The goals of assessment in RCT therapy are thus to identify the sources and functions of the relational images, including controlling societal images, and coping strategies that have shaped the client's experience and to establish the basis for the therapeutic relationship. Although many situations require a diagnosis, RCT therapy has raised questions about traditional diagnoses and has proposed an assessment that, in particular, moves away from personality disorder diagnoses (American Psychiatric Association, 2013; Jordan, 2004; Kaplan, 1983; Nabar, 2011; Stein, 2010). Rather than paying attention to personality traits, RCT therapy recommends that assessment focus on relational dynamics and patterns of chronic disconnections, taking into account the way the larger social context shapes a person's development.

RELATIONAL–CULTURAL ASSESSMENT TOOLS

Several tools have been developed to assess relational health, perceived mutuality, and connection–disconnection (Frey, 2013; Frey, Beesley, & Miller, 2006; Frey, Beesley, & Newman, 2005; Frey, Tobin, & Beesley, 2004; Genero, Miller, & Surrey, 1992; Liang, Tracy, Kenny, Brogan, & Gatha, 2010; Liang, Tracy, Taylor, & Williams, 2002; Liang, Tracy, Taylor, Williams, Jordan, et al., 2002; Tantillo & Sanftner, 2010a).

In the process of assessing clients, and throughout the therapeutic relationship, it is important for therapists to develop an awareness of their own strategies of disconnection, including when they get activated and how they affect each particular therapy relationship. Similarly, it is helpful if the therapist develops some self-awareness about her or his own relational images, particularly where they are fixed and stuck. Therapists need to develop sensitivity to the signs of disconnection in therapy: Is there a drop in energy or a negative affect that may not make sense? Is there fear, dissociation, difficulty talking, or strong and sudden anger? Although the therapist may not always know what is producing the shift, it is sometimes helpful to note, "Something feels like it just shifted here. Did you notice anything?" The assessment phase is useful for beginning to develop this sensitivity and awareness. It is not the therapist's job to pursue or force connection, and thus it is important to be gentle and tentative in all these explorations. Throughout this stage and the entire therapy relationship, monitoring issues of safety and helping to establish the therapy relationship as a safe, growth-promoting context is an ongoing responsibility of the therapist.

THE FLOW OF THERAPY: HEALING RELATIONSHIPS

RCT appreciates that therapy unfolds in a complex and often unpredictable way. Initially the therapy relationship must become "safe enough" to allow the exposure and exploration of vulnerability. With the client, the therapist explores what might get in the way of asking for support and affirms the original wisdom of the client's existing strategies of disconnection. Therapists should not try to dismantle these strategies of disconnection but rather take a respectful approach to them, appreciating their necessity. Over time, therapist and client will begin to question whether these strategies indeed currently support the client's well-being. This period of therapy can be difficult and can last a long time if there has been significant neglect or violation in early relationships. When, over time, the therapy relationship does not replicate the pain of earlier relationships, relational discrepancies are experienced and noticed, and change becomes possible. The client's new understanding of her or his own and others' contribution to the relationship becomes more nuanced and differentiated.

One day Lisa, a client with posttraumatic stress disorder (PTSD), saw frustration in my face and asked, "Do you just want to throw me out or maybe kill me?" Because we had experienced other crises like this, she could hear me when I answered that I was indeed feeling frustrated but in no way did I want to throw her out or kill her, and that, if anything, my frustration made me get a little too intense about trying to understand better. She could see that I was not her rageful father who had repeatedly assaulted her when he was angry. Her relational images were beginning to shift, and a more differentiated experience of affect was coming into being.

As the client comes to expect more authentic and safe connection, she or he begins to take small risks in the area of dealing with the inevitable conflicts that occur in relationships. Rather than moving into avoidance or inauthenticity, the client may begin to try out stating a difference or disagreement. Clients develop more relational confidence and resilience. Relational confidence involves seeing that one has the capacity to move another person, effect a change in a relationship, or affect the well-being of all participants in the relationship. The negative relational images that have limited the client to an expectation that she does not "matter," that she cannot have an impact, and that she is relationally incompetent begin to alter when she sees her own relational competence emerge. Seeing, feeling, and knowing the experience of impact on the therapist moves the client back into relationship.

Relational awareness or mindfulness involves bringing a kind of attunement and consciousness to relationships themselves in addition to each participant in the relationship. Questions such as "What does the relationship need?" "How strong is the relationship?" and "What will support the relationship?" begin to be important. Getting through things together is part of the work, and staying in the uncertainty of the process is more easily said than done. One useful therapy mantra is "listening with engaged curiosity rather than reaching for certainty."

I remember when Lisa, who was extremely critical of me even after we had established a good record of working through disconnections, walked into my office one day and said,

> This has been a pretty tough relationship for both of us, hasn't it? I remember when you called my sister by the wrong name, and I decided that was it, we were done. I said you were losing your marbles or maybe you just didn't care. And you sputtered an apology that I tried to believe. And then remember when I told you later that you weren't the smartest therapist I'd ever had but you weren't the dumbest? And I thought I was giving you a present with that? Yeah, we've been through a lot and we're still here talking to each other. . . . Amazing. I guess we both deserve some credit for that!

This acknowledgment was, in itself, a therapeutic milestone.

Together, over time, the therapist and client create a relationship in which the client can include more of herself, her experience, and her feelings, especially those parts of her experience that she has had to keep out of relationship. The therapist is empathic with how terrifying it is for the client to express yearnings for connection and relinquish strategies to stay out of connection. In therapy with an emotionally present therapist who is committed to responsively reworking relational failures, isolation lessens and the brain changes. In what RCT refers to as *corrective relational experiences*, in which relational images are reworked, it is highly likely that neuronal shifts occur as well (see Chapter 5, this volume).

It is also useful if the therapist can grasp how therapy actually "threatens" a client's strategies of disconnection. It is essential that the therapist appreciate how dangerous it feels to the client to give up these strategies of disconnection; without them, she or he may feel powerless and out of control. The therapist works on being empathic with the central relational paradox, in which the client at once yearns to move into authentic, safe relationship and fears relinquishing the strategies of disconnection to do so. Supported vulnerability occurs in a context that encourages taking the small risks necessary to engage in mutual connection. Vulnerability and openness to being affected are essential to mutuality. The push–pull between opening and protectively closing down can sometimes result in an impasse. When such an impasse occurs, the therapist needs to refocus on following the client's lead and help titrate the movement toward connection appropriately, in such a way that the client is not triggered into fear, or even terror, by a sense of overwhelming, unsafe vulnerability. We support the client in assessing risk: Which relationships offer more safety and which might in fact lead to rewounding?

RCT psychotherapy outcomes include greater freedom to express yearnings for connection without feeling helpless. Strategies for staying out of connection decrease. The client experiences greater confidence in her or his capacity to bear her or his feelings, knowing that she or he need not be alone. Complex feelings and cognitions replace "all-or-nothing" functioning. Pathological certainty shifts. The client develops an enlarged sense of relational resources in her or his life. Feeling connected and empowered, the client begins to experience more of the "five good things": zest, clarity, worth, productivity, and desire for more connection. Thus, as the client's relational skill shifts, her or his energy can move into productive and creative work.

Because RCT therapy enhances the client's desire for connection, it is an approach that is intrinsically about building networks and community. With an appreciation of the sociopolitical forces that create chronic disconnection and disempowerment, the individual often feels empowered to begin to challenge limiting social conditions (Gilligan, Rogers, & Tolman, 1991). Thus, RCT therapy does not simply aim to help people "adjust" to disempowering social circumstances. Such an approach would support the notion that the problem is "in the individual," a model of thinking intrinsically embedded in "separation psychology." Rather, by naming destructive social practices, empathizing with the impossibility of making change alone, reinforcing the importance of finding allies and examining ways to resist shaming practices at both a collective and personal level, RCT therapy supports skills that create both personal well-being and social justice. In her work with African American adolescent girls, Janie V. Ward (2000) provided a beautiful model for building this resistance to isolating and disempowering cultural forces. In lessening isolation and shame, energy becomes available for building more enlivening connections and constructive community (Gilligan et al., 1991).

In sum, compared with many therapeutic approaches, RCT therapy does not offer a vast array of specific techniques. Its major contributions to the therapist's toolbox are its insistence on the use of mutual empathy and radical respect for the client and its emphasis on understanding and reworking chronic disconnections and dysfunctional relational images. The therapy relationship itself creates healing and change.

THE ELEMENTS OF THERAPY

Working With Connections and Disconnections

A *disconnection* occurs in an interaction when one person does not feel heard, understood, or responded to by another person, and there is a loss of empathic responsiveness. Disconnections occur all the time in relationships. Most of them are minor, and they can often become places to work on building stronger connection. If the hurt or "injured" person can represent her or his feelings to the other person and be responded to empathically, acute disconnection leads to stronger connection. Working toward reconnection requires a commitment to better understanding and the effort of repair. If therapists become invested in maintaining images of themselves as totally empathic, caring healers, or people who have moved beyond the human condition of uncertainty, suffering, and stumbling in their own journeys, they will undoubtedly abandon clients at their moments of greatest honesty and vulnerability. When a client takes the risk of voicing a criticism or doubt about the therapist, the therapist who needs to be right or "in control" may well resort to a distancing or demeaning understanding of this honesty, such as "She's confusing me with her father," "He's resisting my interpretation," or "She's expressing her hostility toward me." It is always easier for therapists to bring their empathy to bear on the clients' experience when the clients' hurt is from others. When therapists themselves are the source of the injury, they must make a special effort to avoid defensiveness and thus blame or abandon the client. ✕ *defensiveness.*

RCT therapy suggests that when therapists learn that their misattunements are part of a disconnection, they need to try hard to stay present and take in whatever the complaint or injury is. This can entail being nondefensive and responding in a manner that affirms the client's experience—that is, offering a response that presumably was not there when the client was hurt or injured by others as a child. Thus, the therapist might apologize for failures in memory or lapses in attention or suggest that indeed she or he didn't "get" something and try to go back over it to see how to do better this time. When an empathic failure occurs, the most important question is: What happens next? Is the client offered a relational milieu that says that understanding the client and the client's healing is more important than the therapist's pride or ego? Is the therapist dedicated to really understanding and being with the client's experience? If the therapist sends the message that she or he can receive and work on feedback about her or his own limitations and fallibility, then chronic disconnection need not ensue. Unlike in past relationships, clients do not have to go into shame or protective inauthenticity but can stay with their own experience as the therapist stays with them. This relational repair brings about healing and rekindles hope.

Vignette: The Struggle to Stay Connected

Diana, a 20-year-old woman, was one of my most challenging clients and also one of my most valued teachers. She had been in treatment with several therapists before she arrived at my office. While some of her therapists "gave up on her," she had fired others for being too "shrinky and cold." At that time, I was practicing in a psychiatric teaching hospital where Diana was hospitalized. She began treatment with some hope and also caution. It didn't take her long to find me disappointing. She found me far too conventional and "stiff." She also was quick to notice the ways that I didn't "get" her. In response to my empathic failures, Diana would call her former therapists to report on the latest "dumb" thing I had said. Many of these therapists happened to be esteemed former supervisors of mine. Diana was an accurate recorder of my mistakes, so when I would encounter one of these people in the cafeteria or elsewhere, they would let me know that she had called and then ask, with some surprise, if I had really said such and such (with a roll of the eyes to indicate how ridiculous it would have been if I had). Of course, I had.

I was filled with a sense of shame, exposure, and some irritation that Diana was exposing my failings to so many people. My images of myself as a kind, empathic therapist were being substantially challenged. I had to struggle with my own tendency to disconnect. I was defensive and had little understanding of her pattern of doing this. At first I traveled the traditional route of seeing her actions as being about her veiled hostility toward me. I tried to get her to talk about this. Mostly, I think, I was trying to find a way to get her to stop exposing my incompetence. But over time, I came to appreciate that Diana had developed an intelligent and effective way to stay in treatment with me. For her as a trauma survivor, therapy behind closed doors, where she was invited to share her vulnerability with a powerful other person, was in no way a safe situation. In fact, it was triggering. She had been sexually abused, behind closed doors, by a supposedly trustworthy powerful person (her stepfather). The therapy situation did not offer her safety. Each time I made a mistake or failed her empathically, she experienced an "amygdala hijack." In other words, what might have been perceived as a small error by others signaled to her that she was unsafe and that potentially she would be violated. Thus, that small error caused a big reaction.

In response to this reaction, Diana did something brilliant. She brought the therapy out from behind the closed doors and said, "Listen to this. Look at this. Look at what my therapist is saying and doing. Witness this relationship." In this way, she could feel safe enough to stay in the work. While I struggled with this dynamic and was blind to its meaning for way too long, I finally did understand that she was indeed doing what she had to do to overcome the terror that the situation created for her. When I finally could appreciate this with her and demonstrated that I could get beyond my own uncertainty, shame, and sense of exposure to stay with her needs and help her be safe, she began to feel safe enough to trust that we would work on the misunderstandings and failures together; she no longer had to go into high alert when an empathic failure occurred. But she also knew that if she needed to bring in witnesses, she had that option.

Together Diana and I built enough trust to take the next step of talking together about the hurts, disappointments, and disconnections she experienced in therapy with me. She contributed a great deal to establishing a relationship that was safe enough for both of us that we could facilitate her healing.

The therapist's ability to work with disconnections—those occurring in the therapy and outside it—is crucial to the movement of the therapy. Importantly, the therapist does not want to abandon people to their repetitive expectations of nonresponsiveness from others or push them toward connection when connections have not been experienced as safe. Both the desire to connect and the strategies of disconnection that have developed to protect an individual's vulnerability in a nonempathic milieu must be honored. The therapist must attend carefully to the disconnections in therapy and be ready to renegotiate them to effectively expand the possibility for future change. Sometimes this means pointing out a particular pattern of disconnection; sometimes it means quietly allowing retreat from vulnerability, without a word. For in those moments of extreme vulnerability, there is the possibility that any comment could be perceived as shaming. When the therapist hurts the client—whether through thoughtlessness, misunderstanding, or defensiveness—the hurt must be addressed, with acknowledgment and sometimes an apology, conveying a clear sense that it is not okay for the therapist to hurt the client but also pointing out that such misunderstandings may be inevitable at times. Often the therapist needs to show the pain she or he feels at having created pain for the client.

Contrary to the commonly expressed fear that showing this will lead to a constriction of feeling or will invite the client to "take care of the therapist," this open acknowledgment often leads to a sense that the therapist cares and is strong enough to show her or his vulnerability.

People who suffer with chronic disconnection and hold negative relational images often misattribute blame to themselves for their isolation. They feel in some way defective, that they have caused the isolation, that they are bad or boring or not deserving of love. So it is especially important that therapists take appropriate responsibility for their contributions to disconnections.

Once in therapy, I was a bit preoccupied with a project I was working on. A client I had been seeing for some time was talking about how important writing in her journal was. But as I listened, I couldn't really follow her, and I was feeling a bit lost. I commented, "Things seem to be getting unclear in here today." She quickly responded, "With you or with me?" In that moment she helped me see that my own drifting attention was leaving her feeling alone, and in that isolation she was beginning to slip away. I acknowledged that I thought I was a bit preoccupied, that she had probably been feeling like I had left her alone, and that perhaps a journal was a more reliable place to communicate. It was not necessary to say what exactly preoccupied me; this is part of the difference between experiential validation and full disclosure.

When a disconnection occurs, whatever the relationship has been or is moving toward shifts. There is uncertainty. Accompanying uncertainty is often anxiety and fear. It is a moment of possibility and risk. This moment can be an opportunity to forge stronger connection or to close down around pain and fear. When there is nonresponsiveness, a holding of images of what should be, or clinging to some illusion of certainty, therapist and client move out of the open space of relatedness into guarding their separateness or self-images. When the situation is indeed unsafe, this represents appropriate protectiveness. If people cannot take the small risks to test out how safe the relationship would be for open curiosity and learning, they cannot move toward each other. When images of how we "should be" begin to take over, real relationship suffers (this is true for therapists as well). Preoccupation with self-image replaces attunement to the other person and the relationship. Questions to ask include the following: Can we do something about this difficulty in our relationship? Is there sufficient mutuality and safety to undertake the necessary vulnerability to work through the difficulty together? What do I or we need to shift toward supported vulnerability and moving back into safe and growth-enhancing connection? By asking and answering questions like these, therapist and client together build a new template for negotiating hard places in relationship.

Working With Empathy

Empathy is a crucial element in rebuilding positive relational images and creating connection. *Empathy* is a complex cognitive-affective skill; it is the ability to put oneself in the other's shoes, to "feel with" the other, to understand the other's experience. It is crucial to the felt experience of connectedness and is therefore crucial to healing in therapy. It demands clarity of the source of the affect (where does the affect first arise?), and it creates increasing clarity about the meaning of the client's experience. It also lessens the experiential distance between client and therapist. Empathy is not just a means to better understand the client; in mutually empathic exchanges, the isolation of the client is altered. The client feels less alone, more joined with the therapist. Seeing that she has an impact on the therapist, she begins to believe that she is relationally competent and that she matters. It is likely that in these moments of empathy and resonance, there is active brain resonance between therapist and client, which can alter the landscape and functioning of the brain (Banks, 2016; Schore, 1994). Thus, those areas of the brain that register isolation and exclusion fire less, and those areas that indicate empathic responsiveness begin to activate. The orbitofrontal cortex is quite plastic and subject to relational reworking throughout most of life. Empathic responsiveness in therapy can help develop new neuronal pathways and shift old patterns of firing (Banks, 2016; Cozolino, 2014; Doidge, 2007).

Mutual empathy is based on the notion that for empathy to "make a difference" and create healing and lessen isolation, the client must be able to see, know, and feel the therapist's empathic response. Chronic disconnection leads to demoralization and a loss of hope for empathic responsiveness from the other person—indeed, from all others. Only by bringing oneself more fully into empathic relationship can one learn new responses and begin to discard the old, fixed, overly generalized expectations of relational failure.

Mutual empathy, based in respect, allows both people to see the impact they have on one another. The therapist's responsiveness to the client's feelings gives the latter a firsthand experience of being "felt" (*really* understood) by the other, of having impact. When the client is tearfully recounting her mother's painful death and notices that the therapist, too, is tearing up, she knows her pain is received and felt, that her suffering matters. The client feels less isolated and hopeless. Whereas in prior relationships, the client may have felt closed down and not responded to, she or he now sees how she or he emotionally affects the other person. There is a deepening sense of trust in these exchanges—in oneself, in the other, and in the relationship—and an expanding belief in the possibility that relationships and individuals can make a difference in the surrounding world. The client's cognitive capacities also come alive, with more clarity and creativity. Finding growth-fostering relationships does not lead to withdrawal from the world in a cocoon of warm and gratifying connection. Rather, it leads to an increased investment in the world and in others' well-being.

The *separate-self model* overemphasizes the "taking in" of supplies and the building of a separate sense of well-being. RCT contends that one's own growth need not be pitted against another's; participating in growth-fostering relationships enables mutual growth. Empathy for oneself and others is enlarged. We do not have to choose between selfishness and self-lessness; mutuality provides another pathway, one that benefits all people in their interactions. Overly personalized and distorted understandings of past relationships begin to shift when we can embrace this more expansive understanding of relational growth.

A client who had been verbally abused by her mother and who had taken her mother's rejection as a sign that she was "bad" began to see that her mother was limited by her own history of abuse and neglect. As she developed more accurate empathy with her mother, she began to see that her mother's treatment of her had more to do with her mother's limitations than her own badness. This allowed her to begin to relinquish a sense of herself as bad, annoying, and unlovable. As she developed a more accurate understanding of her mother, she also began to develop self-empathy. Where once she experienced self-loathing and self-rejection, she began to understand herself as a very small, young child who could not possibly grasp the reasons for her mother's abusive behavior. She felt sadness and a sense of anger that her mother could not have been a better mother, but she no longer assumed she was the problem, the cause of the abandonment.

Usually, we think of empathy as directed toward others, but it is also possible to direct empathy toward one's own experience, something termed *self-empathy* in RCT (Jordan, 1983). The development of self-empathy is a major source of change in therapy. In self-empathy, the client begins to bring an empathic awareness and presence to bear on her or his own experience. Thus, rather than judging, criticizing, or rejecting her or his own feelings, the client begins to stay with them, to be empathic with how they came about. Self-empathy is a powerful tool in working with shame and disconnection. When faced with a client who is particularly self-critical or is expressing self-loathing, the therapist may gently ask questions about how the client might view this situation if it involved a best friend or family member instead of her or him. If a client is blaming herself for a failure to stand up to her bullying brother as a child, the therapist might ask her to imagine herself at that age and recognize how small and vulnerable she was.

In working with trauma survivors who lack self-empathy, it is often helpful to include participation in a PTSD group at some point in the course of recovery. In these groups, the empathy that is not directed toward one's own experience of abuse is often available to others. Thus, abuse survivors will "get" how small and vulnerable another abuse survivor was when she or he was violated and will respond with great empathy. Over time, they begin to appreciate their similarity to this other person and find empathy for themselves as a child or as an adult having to deal with the pain, loss, and shame of childhood trauma. Thus, in these groups, empathy for others generates self-empathy. Sometimes other group members will actively encourage the capacity for self-empathy, making comments such as, "Diane, you're so caring and empathic with Kelly when she's talking about her abuse, but you're so hard on yourself! Do you see that?"

Developing empathy for one's own experience and for the other person does not involve subordinating or abandoning one's own experience to the other. Rather, RCT facilitates movement out of the dichotomous world of self versus other and selfishness versus selflessness. Empathy for the other also does not involve condoning or accepting the validity of another's hurtful behavior. Rather, it involves the discovery—and relief in discovery—that the other's personal limitations drove her or his hurtful behavior. This leads to significant shifts in relational images and acceptance of one's intrinsic worth that lie at the heart of growth in relationship. Recently there has been an interest in self-compassion, which is akin to self-empathy (Germer, 2009; Neff, 2011). Both are anchored in a nonjudgmental, kind attitude toward oneself. Self-empathy involves not just providing a loving attitude toward oneself but also a kind of understanding and "staying with" the truth of one's experience. Compassion taps into the desire to end suffering, offering the intentionality of altering pain through caring and sending *metta* or loving energy. Self-empathy provides both kindness and understanding (e.g., "As I forgive myself and stay with my feelings, I 'get' why I am feeling this way. It makes sense, and I can accept how this came to be. No need for blame, just notice the shut down and offer acceptance instead."). Self-empathy is never about curtailing empathy for others; self-empathy is in the service of building the possibility for mutual empathy. Without the capacity for self-empathy, finding empathy for others, for the relationship, and for the limitations that we all have is not possible.

Working With Relational Images

The relinquishing and modification of negative relational images through the process of mutual empathy and self-empathy is one of the central pathways of change in RCT therapy. Therapist and client work together with the obstacles that get in the way of the yearning for safe connection. In the process the client becomes more present and responsive in current relationships.

In addition to using the power of mutual empathy to begin to deconstruct limiting relational images, the therapist looks for the discrepant relational images, those images that may contain a different, more positive message or create a different expectation. For instance, a primary relational image for a client might be that if she expresses her strong spirit or anger, she will be rejected as "bad," an image that arose in her relationship with her parents. But she may have had an uncle who enjoyed her high energy and her outspoken anger. This discrepant relational image ("When I'm feisty, my uncle seems to get a kick out of me and supports me.") may become the building block for reconnecting with those aspects of her experience that opposed injustice or could tolerate conflict. As the client begins to test the discrepant images, more experience accrues to them, and they become represented more fully in current relationships. When a person is making such changes, it is always important to assist in differentiating which relationships are "safe" and welcoming of these experiences and which may in fact reinforce the old limiting images. Because people tend to be drawn to the familiar, we may often find ourselves in relationships with people who confirm our old, fixed relational images. It is important that the therapist not be a Pollyanna, leading the client to believe that all relationships will be welcoming and supportive of these new patterns. Often the therapist will have to help the client develop strategies about how to effectively and safely bring new relational expectations into the world. It is easier to shift these images when beginning a new relationship, but it is often necessary to introduce changes into existing relationships where the other person may in fact resist such movement. The therapist can help the client titrate these changes.

In the therapy relationship itself, the client has an opportunity to reexamine, question, and rework relational images. Thus, an adult who developed the relational image "When I need something, my vulnerability exposes me to physical abuse" may begin to learn in therapy a competing relational image: "When I need something, my needs are respected, and there is a possibility that I can find a way to get them safely met." In therapy, the pathological certainty of the negative relational images can be met with a question and the possibility of a different outcome. Relational hope begins to grow. Under these conditions, clients begin slowly and carefully to relinquish strategies of disconnection, which in turn generates an increased sense of possibility, although that possibility is often accompanied by a sense of vulnerability. The therapist's capacity for authentic presence and responsiveness at these times can be particularly reassuring. Trust enlarges as the client takes small steps toward more connection in a context that respects her wariness about such moves.

THERAPIST RESPONSIVENESS AND AUTHENTICITY

Offering a reliable, open presence to the client, the therapist's cognitive and emotional responsiveness, which is at the core of mutual empathy, contributes to the relaxation of old patterns and fears. As the client changes, the therapist will be changing too. Jean Baker Miller (2002) noted that "if growth is to occur in any relationship, both—or all—of the people involved have to change" (p. 4). RCT suggests that all change must be mutual and involves an enlarging circle of mutuality. In therapy, both people are affected, although not in the same way; the therapist is there to facilitate change in the client. Not only does the client have to access vulnerability, but the therapist too must be open to being affected and changed, even vulnerable. At the same time, the therapist, like the client, must also feel safe. It is the therapist's "job" to be there for the client and for the relationship, to facilitate change. This is not simply an everyday relationship of reactivity and spontaneity. The therapist has a role, responsibilities, a code of ethics, and the precious task of helping the client navigate her or his vulnerability and hopefulness. The therapist must exercise clinical judgment at all times.

Many therapists get caught in the mistaken thought that strength and safety arise from the therapist being authoritative, showing that she or he is "above," in control, powerful, perfect. Proponents of RCT would argue that strength arises in building good connection and that, paradoxically, vulnerability in relationship is necessary to the experience of strength and courage. Courage is not something that is built in isolation; rather, it grows in relationship, through the encouragement of others, by being strongly anchored in relationship (Jordan, 1990). The capacity to move and be moved by the other person grows as healing progresses (Eldridge, Surrey, Rosen, & Miller, 2008).

The therapist creates a relational context, which includes her authenticity and presence (Boatwright & Nolan, 2006; Miller et al., 1997). This therapeutic authenticity provides important relational information to the client (e.g., "I can begin to see my impact on others," "I feel less out of control and I feel that I matter.") Rather than fearing that emotional responsiveness will derail the therapeutic process, RCT therapy suggests that this responsiveness is essential to the healing of patterns of relational disconnection and negative relational images. Responsiveness does not require that the therapist share all her life experiences or all spontaneous emotional reactions during the therapy. Instead, a judicious use of emotional transparency and anticipatory empathy allows the client to begin to understand her or his impact on the therapist and hence on other people. Responsiveness differs from reactivity, total transparency, or kneejerk (amygdala) authenticity. It is modulated and attuned to the well-being of the other person. Therapists trained in more traditional, opaque practices may have to learn how best to use therapist authenticity for the benefit of the client. Sparks (2009) wrote a personal chronicle of her own developing understanding and use of authenticity as she embraced an RCT approach to doing therapy.

Traditional analytically derived psychodynamic therapies emphasize the importance of working with transference (Freud, 1957; Gill, 1983; Racker, 1953). Although few therapists today would espouse the development of a transference neurosis or the maintenance of a classical "blank screen" approach, the roots of these biases remain in many therapy models. With these biases, emotional responsiveness on the part of the therapist is thought to be potentially damaging. Although a totally spontaneous, reactive therapist would indeed compromise the safety and therapy of clients, a *responsive* therapist, holding the well-being and growth of the client at the center of the work (and adhering to ethical standards), provides useful data to someone struggling with isolation and negative relational expectations. Clinical judgment always informs the responsiveness that comes into the room. Irene Stiver used to speak of finding the "one true thing" that could be said that would be helpful. This did not imply there was one true or magical thing to be said but was meant to guide the therapist to stay in the realm of therapeutic authenticity. There has to be an appreciation that client and therapist occupy different roles and are in differing places of vulnerability and power. The therapist's job is to help the client and to protect the relationship and the safety of both people in the relationship. Mutuality in therapy does not imply equality of power or sameness of role.

There are times when the therapist should not call attention to her or his responsiveness. For instance, tears in response to the pain a client is describing can provide important feedback, but sometimes those tears can create discomfort or fear and not be useful. In judging how and when to use empathic transparency, the therapist is constantly guided by these questions: Will this facilitate growth? Will this further the healing? In assessing when and how to share her realness, the therapist is using something we call *anticipatory empathy.* This involves anticipating the response of the other based on the emotional knowledge one has gained of the client in therapy. Having listened and observed, the therapist develops an emotional sense of how different things will affect the client. Along with a "sense" that the therapist has in the moment of how the client is responding, the history of the client's reactions informs the therapist's response. Authenticity in therapy depends on thoughtful use of anticipatory empathy. The therapist uses her or his responses to help the client feel less isolated and more effective. After offering a response, the therapist carefully watches the impact it has on the client, which in turn helps shape the next response.

Errors in anticipatory empathy can certainly occur. It is not the therapist's job to be perfectly empathic at all times. Empathic failures can be painfully blatant (e.g., "You're the only client I work with who has said sometimes my attention drifts. What do you think that's about for you?") or more subtle (e.g., the therapist thinks, "This client is not really angry at me but this is a projection of her anger at her mother."). It doesn't have to be either–or. It may be that the client is really angry with the therapist and the therapist has done something to stir up this anger. It may also be that there are some important roots of similar anger in past relationships. When the therapist is open to both possibilities, clients often feel less judged or shamed. What matters is how the therapist responds in the face of her or his own empathic failures. Does the therapist encourage the client to notice these failures and represent feelings of hurt or anger over them, or does she move into a defensive and self-protective mode? A different kind of therapist might think, "I didn't really miss that point, she's just not able to hear it. She's 'resistant.'" This stance can feel dismissive to the client and may actually contribute to lack of movement in the treatment. When the therapist climbs into theory and certainty, instead of responding empathically to the specific client, her or his specific history, and the specific moment, the therapist often emotionally abandons the client.

Vignette: Responsiveness of the Therapist

Barbara was a 24-year-old, well-educated White woman who had seen six therapists before she began treatment with me. Each therapy had an unhappy demise, often following an impasse where Barbara felt unseen, unheard, and angry. She had initiated the ending of all but two of these treatments. In those two cases, her therapists "gave up" and suggested she was not treatable. Barbara had been diagnosed at various times as having schizophrenia, borderline personality disorder, and bipolar disorder. She led an extremely isolated life. At the time I began treating her, she was hospitalized for a failed suicide attempt.

Barbara came to me with a modicum of hope (she had heard I was a little less "rigid" than some of the other therapists), but she held no great expectations. Early on she decided that I was not much better than the other clinicians she had seen. The early weeks of treatment were characterized by long silences, occasional talking about her previous therapists, and some genuine expressions of fear that this would be no more helpful than anything else she had tried. I did not press her to give up her fears, acknowledged it had been a hard road, and told her that although I could not guarantee that I would understand her any better than the others, I was committed to trying. I also suggested she had no real reason to trust me.

One day she came to a session with fresh blood on her shirt, having recently scratched her arm. She wanted to know if I would "fire" her. I said her self-injury was very difficult for me to see. She wondered in a challenging way if I was worried about what my colleagues would think when they saw someone coming into my office with blood dripping down her arm. I hesitated and agreed that the thought had crossed my mind, but that I also could see she was in real pain and needed to be able to communicate that to me. She looked at first triumphant (at my admission of personal concern about my "reputation") but then genuinely relieved (perhaps that

I had spoken a piece of truth about myself that she knew anyway). We then had a truly collaborative conversation about how she might be able to really let me know her pain and whether she could trust my response.

Soon after this incident, Barbara began to talk about childhood sexual abuse at the hands of an uncle and how no one, particularly her mother, had believed her when she attempted to tell her about it. She had not revealed this abuse in any of her previous therapies. After her disclosure, she became extremely agitated and again mute. I allowed her distance. When she began to speak again, it was to criticize almost everything about me: "You aren't strong enough. You're too detached. You're not available when I need you. You're wishy-washy. You don't really care about me. You are among the worst of the therapists I have seen." I sometimes felt reactive, and sometimes I was defensive. Once I got angry and told her how frustrated I felt, that I was trying so hard to be there for her and nothing I did seemed good enough. Then I had to apologize for blaming her. I worried about her sometimes when I was at home, and I told her so. Then I regretted telling her.

Despite my own difficulty practicing what I preached (responsive, nondefensive presence with her connections and disconnections), slowly we navigated our way through her pain, isolation, and terror. It was largely around the failures and, paradoxically, the increasing closeness with her subsequent leaps into angry isolation that we began to experience movement and shifts. After 2 years of a highly volatile therapy, things began to settle down. The prevailing relational images that told her any increasing vulnerability on her part would lead to abuse and violation by others began to shift. She could begin to entertain the possibility that if she showed her "real" feelings, she would be responded to empathically and cared about. Her reactivity began to alter so that when the inevitable empathic failures happened, she could feel angry and disappointed rather than alarmed, terrified, or rageful.

Barbara's life was taking shape too. After years of working in marginal and poorly paid positions, she landed a high-level job, realized she was attracted to women, and started dating a kind and caring woman.

She began to bring humor into the therapy, and the two of us laughed together over some of the predicaments we had lived through. I developed incredible respect for the ways she had learned to keep herself safe and the ways she had helped us stay in relationship. My realness was important to her. She was incredibly sensitive to inauthenticity and "playing games," and she felt there was "a lot of that in most therapies." Eventually I "got" that she needed to be vigilant to my lapses in empathy; each failure on my part made her feel unsafe, as if she was too vulnerable and about to be further injured by me. Together we worked on ways to achieve safety so that both of us did not feel whiplashed. When, toward the end of therapy, we reflected together on how the therapy had been, she commented on my willingness to be vulnerable with her. Barbara felt that had made a real difference; it made me less dangerous to her.

When I acknowledged my limitations ("stating my limits," sharing how I could or could not be responsive in a particular interaction) instead of "setting limits" for her (which implies the client is wrongly "asking for too much"), she felt respected. She wondered,

> Isn't it ironic that when you showed yourself as most fallible and vulnerable, I had the most trust in you? You didn't always get it right . . . and often it took awhile for you to get it at all, but you almost always came back, trying and clearly imperfect. That made you feel safe to me.

Although the vulnerability each of us experienced was informed by the roles we held (therapist and client), there was ultimately a mutual openness to change and mutual vulnerability that was crucial for the therapeutic process. For those who are trained in separate-self paradigms, this concept of mutuality in therapy may invoke images of "boundary violation." In contrast to the knee-jerk use of terms like *boundary issues*, which arise in separate-self therapeutic models, RCT therapy explicitly attends to the safety of the client and specifically delineates and pays attention to the issues that are covered by the boundary concept. Thus, RCT therapy notes the importance of (a) establishing safety by building good connections rather than by exercising power over others; (b) establishing clarity, especially about whose experience is whose; and (c) being able to say no in interpersonal situations, to maintain a sense of comfort and safety for both client and therapist. This is referred to in RCT therapy as *stating limits* rather than *setting limits*. Setting limits often arises in an unequal power relationship and can be accompanied by some condescension or judgment about the behaviors or needs that are being limited, while stating one's personal limits gives information that is important in any relationship.

Issues of safety, clarity, and relational regulation are at the heart of most concepts of "boundaries," but without elucidation the boundary concept can be used in a readily predictable way to maintain therapist distance and support "power over" dynamics. In contrast, creating growth by fostering safe connection is a core concern of RCT therapy. RCT practitioners have a strong commitment to protecting clients from exploitation by therapists who are using clients for their own needs. Furthermore, negotiating safety, clarity, and limits in relationships provides important relational information. Attention to these factors helps clients learn how to notice relationship dynamics. Working with "boundary issues" in RCT therapy is thus driven by a need to learn and become more relationally competent rather than by a need to impose limits or control the client. Both therapist and client learn in these interactions. When boundaries are conceptualized only as protective barriers against the outside and serve as significant markers of a separate self and power over others, they often serve to maintain and enforce the existing power arrangements.

Often therapists move to a position of distancing, labeling, and attempting to control when they feel they must be the expert, certain and in charge, particularly in the face of a sense of helplessness or uncertainty. RCT therapy suggests therapy is actually characterized by *fluid expertise* and mutuality. Fluid expertise recognizes that both people in the therapy relationship have expertise they use to move the treatment forward. Although some worry that mutuality in this relationship renders it less safe, RCT therapy argues that by building respectful, healing connections in which both people are open to being affected, we in fact make it safer rather than more hazardous for the client. For change to occur, therapists must learn to be present, open to vulnerability, and to being truly affected by the client. Such presence does not devolve into wallowing in "not knowing" or reactivity but allows openness to being affected by another's words or state. This responsiveness is at the heart of all relational movement. In essence, the therapist implies: "I am moved by you and you see, know and feel that you have had an impact on me. You (client) 'get' that you matter, you are relationally effective, you can be empathized with and responded to. You are not alone, and you are not helpless."

Mutuality depends on shared vulnerability and openness to change, but it does not indicate sameness of role or symmetry in disclosure. When a client inquires about information that a therapist feels is "private," the therapist might decide not to answer a particular question. It may be important to indicate that the question is perfectly natural but that the therapist is not comfortable with that disclosure. Conflict can ensue and, if welcomed by the therapist, can contribute to real growth. Sometimes clients feel they need to adjust the parameters of treatment in some way that feels uncomfortable to the therapist. In such situations, it is the therapist's responsibility to attend deeply to what lies beneath the client's request.

> Susan came to her first session armed with a tape recorder and announced that she needed to tape the sessions. Taken aback, I found myself wondering to myself to what use these tapes would be put. Was she litigious? Would she use them to help her remember what we talked about? Would these tapes one day be in the hands of a colleague who would critically review my interventions? I immediately suggested we needed to be sure we were both comfortable with this arrangement. She quickly retorted that she was quite comfortable, but perhaps I wasn't. I tried hard not to get defensive or pathologize her request. I acknowledged that in fact it made me a bit anxious. I said I wasn't sure what that was about for me, and I would appreciate it if we could talk more about it before we instituted this particular action. She reluctantly agreed. I soon realized I was uneasy about possible exposure. But I also realized that Susan was quite dissociated and that at times she remembered almost nothing about our sessions, so listening to the tapes would be useful for her. After several sessions, I agreed that taping made sense, and as I had an increasing sense of who she was, I felt more comfortable with such an arrangement. It turned out to be quite helpful for her.
>
> A traditional approach could have gotten sidetracked into worrying about how Susan was trying to "manipulate" the therapist or

inappropriately alter the boundaries. The biggest downside for me was that she had crystal-clear recall of our previous sessions when she arrived, and sometimes I had to struggle to catch up with her. But it was worth it.

"social suffering"

ACKNOWLEDGING THE POWER OF SOCIAL CONTEXT

RCT practitioners believe in the validation of the client's experience, including naming the power of contextual factors to create psychological suffering. RCT therapy pays particular attention to the effects of privilege, racism, sexism, classism, and heterosexism. This includes acknowledging all the ways that our contexts affect us. The impact of the larger culture on both therapist and client is dramatic: We all carry the wounds or privileges of cultural forces. Too often therapists personalize wounds and difficulties that are rooted in sociocultural pain. Thus, someone struggling with the impact of racism may be treated as paranoid or untrusting. The tendency to blame the victim can be rampant in a system that does not adequately take into account the suffering caused by systemic marginalization and oppression. If we constantly work only at the individual level of understanding, we become complicit with the existing forces of disconnection and oppression in the culture. We fail our clients and a society that needs healing as well.

By valuing and striving for mutual relationship and by substituting a relational psychology for one that makes systems of dominance normative, RCT becomes a force for social justice. Christina Robb (2006) noted that RCT

> discovered nothing less than the political and psychological power of relationship: the political use of dissociation and disconnection to widen power disparities and keep them wide, and the power of personal relationships and cultural connections to balance power and foster growth. (p. xvii)

Robb continued, "It changes everything to see and hear relationships. Not selves" (p. xviii). RCT therapists bring an awareness to their work that is both personal and political, and relational–cultural theorists continue to alter the prevailing paradigms of Western psychology. In therapy the change occurs one relationship at a time, shifting relational and controlling images that limit our capacity to live fully.

Vignette: Controlling Images and Personal Changes

Brenda was a brilliant African American lawyer who was in weekly therapy for a little over a year. She worked in a predominantly White law firm in an environment that often subtly and blatantly turned her into "the problem." She grew up in the South and attended mostly segregated schools. Brenda had been in therapy before and found it helpful. In our first session, she said she wanted to focus on her struggles at work.

She was troubled by the demanding hours of her job and the existence of racist practices that no one else noticed and that she bore in silence. Given these concerns, Brenda wondered early in our first session whether it made sense to see a White therapist. We talked about my limitations in understanding some of her experience and how that might not serve her well. I suggested I could refer her to an African American colleague who I thought was an exceptional clinician. She said she would think about that. I struggled with my own feelings. I liked her already; I would feel sad if she chose not to continue, but I also had to acknowledge my own inevitable racism, the possibility that my racial self-consciousness would get in the way of my being helpful to her, and the very real issue that as much as I could identify with and empathize with many of her experiences of marginalization, I really didn't "get" in a deep way what it is like to live as a Black person in a racist, White-dominated society.

The first time Brenda told me of a situation at work where she was overlooked for an important assignment, I struggled to stay with her racial understanding and not move into a personalized explanation that would have left her as alone and disempowered as she had been at work. I am trained to "go for" the personal understanding, but I had to stay alert to the contextual, cultural, racial, and power issues that were at play and that she was clearly experiencing. I was as ignorant in some ways as her supervisor. I alluded to some work that a colleague was doing about the microaggressions involved in racism—the endless, small, often disavowed ways that attacks are made on the marginalized person's experience and personhood. Brenda listened quietly and then talked about her anger at White people who don't take responsibility for their attitudes, who rush in to support other White people and leave her alone to be the fall guy or the angry Black woman. I assumed I was a part of this insensitive group, but I did not comment on it. I wanted to honor both her trust and her mistrust in me. She knew how limited I was in some ways to truly know her empathically, but she also could see my pain when she shared her pain, and this created the glimmer of a bridge between us.

In the course of therapy, there were personal and cultural misunderstandings. We struggled with controlling images born both of White privilege and of marginalization and oppression. As I listened to Brenda's courageous struggle to find voice at her place of work, I had to recognize and work on my internalized, White, middle-class relational images of being nice and not making trouble (despite my intellectual embrace of the notion of "speaking truth to power"). Brenda had to struggle with her own internalized images that warned her against being "too loud." On one occasion I presumptively suggested I could understand her pain at having to endlessly deal with racism. She looked at me sharply and said, "I seriously doubt any White woman of privilege can get that one." She was right, and I let her know that she was right. I apologized. At times, I tried too hard to demonstrate that I was "different" from other privileged White people when in fact I carry the distortions of racism in my psychological bones as much as anyone raised in this culture. I had to track the impact of my White privilege with more awareness than I was used to.

As we navigated these relational ruptures, teasing apart the personal and sociopolitical, we built a good enough sense of safety in our connection. We talked together about the oppressive impact of controlling images and Brenda's struggle to maintain a positive sense of herself in the midst of this sea of negative expectation. She became less tentative in her depiction of inequities at work and began, increasingly effectively, to point out to her colleagues the ways in which she was overlooked or treated stereotypically. She also became a beacon for other people of color in her office; she found allies and served as an inspiration to some of the younger people of color.   *powerful*

At the conclusion of therapy, Brenda noted that she felt stronger. She continued to work on projects that were meaningful to her and to others, and she was given more appreciation for her contributions at work. She acknowledged that there were places of limitation in our work that were partly about race, and she said she felt sad about that.

I, too, felt this and shared with her my own sadness. I added that I was glad we both had persevered despite what was sometimes a roller coaster of disconnections and that I would miss our meetings.

RCT therapy encourages working across cultural and racial differences, but it also recognizes the challenges that exist for therapist and client in a culture that has been so traumatizing for oppressed groups. All of that history accompanies both people into the therapy setting. Mutual empathy is difficult across difference. When in the larger culture those differences are stratified and become places of judgment and dominance, stretching to meet across distance can feel treacherous. The possibility of inadvertent wounding is always there, and the challenge to really listen and understand freshly is daunting. But mutual empathy with differences is a potential place of great growth and offers an enhanced resilience for all participants. RCT specifically addresses how societal oppression increases disconnections for people from historically marginalized backgrounds (people of color, women, LGBTQ people).

Multiculturalism and social justice principles are central to RCT (Singh & Moss, 2016). RCT notes that heteronormative cultures create relational dilemmas for historically marginalized groups. RCT provides a lens that helps deconstruct heterosexist bias and privilege (Singh & Moss, 2016). RCT challenges existing power-over relational interactions.

BUILDING RELATIONAL RESILIENCE

RCT therapists constantly work with relational resilience within the therapy relationship itself. The idea that growth is not a one-way process is a key aspect of models of relational versus personal resilience. When we think *"the myth of separation"*

of creating internal traits of resilience—of "building a self" or getting "supplies" from the outside to the inside—we are defined by the myth of separation. The culture's emphasis on hyperindividualism and self-importance supports this myth. Thus, most models overlook the very real power of our need to contribute to the well-being of others and to feel useful in that way. Relational resilience takes full account of the context within which one is stressed. It also fully credits the desire to contribute to relationship as well as the need to turn to relationships for support. Resilience is not an internal trait that people carry around with them. Participating in another person's growth is crucial to one's well-being. We are beings who seek mutuality and gain meaning from being a part of and contributing to something larger. Often that "something larger" is a relationship, a community, a social action group, an organization or a sense of "the common good."

Ironically, programs or groups that are often called "self-help" usually involve a high degree of mutual help. Alcoholics Anonymous (AA) is a good example of such a program. From the outside, people usually portray it as about "reaching out for help" or helping yourself—that is, as a self-help group. However, AA and other 12-step programs provide the opportunity to contribute to the well-being of others and hence reestablish a sense of dignity around feeling that one has something to contribute at the same time that one is receiving important support. These are clearly programs characterized by great mutuality and community building. They exemplify the practice of *supported vulnerability*. Many studies of the power of group support overlook the mutuality of these caring groups. For instance, Spiegel's (1991) study of patients with cancer found that those who participated in small groups experienced less anxiety, depression, and pain than those who did not participate; patients participating in small groups also lived twice as long. Clearly, the relationships made a difference. Interpretation of these results emphasized that these patients were *receiving* help from others. However, it is likely that *providing* support, feeling "useful," and feeling that one "matters" also served to enhance their sense of well-being (Spiegel, 1991). The process of mutual empathy stimulates healing and helps us come back into growth fostering connection.

Mutual involvement characterizes resilience in a relational model (Hartling, 2008; Jordan, 2013). Relational resilience depends on developing the ability to move toward others when old patterns of isolation begin to take hold. Realizing that one is deemed valuable by others, that one has something to offer, can be as healing as being the recipient of others' support. The tendency to distort what is helpful about certain treatments (e.g., "getting support") creates blind spots in our understanding of what is truly healing: the participation in mutually empathic connection.

SHORT-TERM THERAPY APPLICATIONS OF RCT THERAPY

The reported use of RCT therapy has been primarily in long-term therapy in which conditions allow a deepening of the work in the therapeutic relationship. Although RCT therapy was not developed for short-term therapy settings, it has in fact been used by many clinicians in short-term focused therapy. A *Consumer Reports* article ("Mental Health: Does Therapy Help?," 1995) indicated that, across theories, the longer the course of therapy, the more improvement that occurred, but in today's world, more and more people are urged or forced by financial or insurance constraints to limit their sessions. Short-term therapy is known for its emphasis on defining goals and creating behavioral shifts. Although short-term models often stress a collaborative relationship between therapist and client, they also tend to focus on "separation" and termination from the outset. Some actually augment the experience of confrontation and anxiety to create change (Davanloo, 1980; Sifneos, 1979). RCT therapy advocates a very different model of short-term work (Jordan, Handel, Alvarez, & Cook-Noble, 2000).

Short-term RCT therapy emphasizes developing relational awareness, getting to know the client's relational patterns and images, and encouraging an appreciation of existing and ongoing resources for connection, such as family and friends. In addition, the client is given tools to build new relationships. The therapist brings the message that we are not meant to function on our own in Lone Ranger fashion (although, in fact, the Lone Ranger was not alone). The ongoing importance of relationships is empha-sized and normalized. The therapist provides an introduction to the neuro-biology of connection and teaches about the ways in which human beings are programmed for connection (Banks, 2016; Lieberman, 2013; Porges, 2011; Siegel, 2010). The value to a person's well-being of involvement in community where one is both helping and being helped is stressed. These messages help deconstruct the cultural imperatives of self-interest, stand-ing on your own two feet, autonomy, and invulnerability. In a collaborative setting, the therapist respects the client's strengths and weaknesses, ability to connect, and need to disconnect. Importantly, the therapist does not stress termination but frames the work as potentially intermittent: One may accomplish a piece of work, decide not to meet for some time, and return if new issues arise or a check-in is desired. This return to therapy is not seen as a sign of weakness or failure but rather as an expected good out-come of a successful therapy. Mental health is not equated with autonomy.

A relational model of time-limited therapy emphasizes connection rather than separation. Often there are several closely spaced sessions to encourage building a sense of connection; subsequently, sessions can be spaced further apart. RCT therapy does not advocate termination as a final, "forever" ending in any therapy; it is especially important to maintain this sense of future connection when doing short-term work. Focusing on two or three core relational patterns that may be causing pain often leads to shifts in the rigidity and pervasiveness of these patterns. One place where RCT therapy has been used effectively on a short-term basis is in col-lege counseling services where short-term therapy is dictated by the high demand for services (Comstock, 2005; Jordan, Handel, Alvarez, & Cook-Noble, 2000; Kopala & Keitel, 2003). A study of brief relational–cultural therapy conducted in a women's treatment center in Toronto found signifi-cant improvement in eight outcome measures; the therapeutic gains were maintained at 3- and 6-month follow-ups (Oakley et al., 2013). Frey (2013) reviewed research on RCT's role in developing counseling competencies and found that it was very helpful to counseling students.

OBSTACLES TO OR DIFFICULTIES
WITH USING RCT THERAPY

The use of RCT therapy has been expanding (Kazlow, 2002). It is increasingly being used in work with couples and families (Jordan & Carlson, 2013), groups, organizations (Fletcher, 1999; Vicario, Tucker, Smith-Adcock, & Hudgins-Mitchell, 2013), and schools (Schwartz & Holloway, 2012; Vicario et al., 2013). It has also been used successfully with a wide range of clients and patients, including those who have been diagnosed as schizophrenic and bipolar, as well as other chronically mentally ill patients and incarcerated women (Coll & Duff, 1995). Vicario et al. (2013) found that relational–cultural play therapy helped reestablish healthy connections with children exposed to trauma in relationships. Banks (2006b) developed a model of trauma therapy based in RCT and psychobiology. Many clinicians have found RCT therapy to be particularly helpful with clients with eating disorders (Sanftner et al., 2006; Tantillo & Sanftner, 2003, 2010b; Trepal, Boie, & Kress, 2012). Specific RCT protocols have also been developed to work with women struggling with substance abuse (Covington, 1999).

The model is effective in working with many diverse clients. However, it is likely that someone entrenched in what is known as a sociopathic pattern of behavior might prove difficult to treat with RCT therapy. With such individuals, the avoidance of personal authenticity and vulnerability is often deeply entrenched and unyielding, and the capacity for empathy may be severely compromised.

Despite the increasing acknowledgment of RCT's therapy contributions, the dominant therapeutic culture, with its emphasis on therapist "neutrality," makes it difficult for therapists from all different approaches to appreciate the importance of therapist responsiveness. RCT therapy suggests that neutrality or objectivity may not actually be achievable and that to the extent it encourages an opaque demeanor on the part of the therapist, it may contribute to disconnection rather than connection. Although many approaches suggest that an authoritative style is best, RCT therapy recommends an appreciation of fluid expertise in which both client and therapist are seen as carrying important wisdom and knowledge. But even when a theory like RCT suggests that authoritative neutrality is not always of use and may in fact be destructive to the therapeutic task, the therapist must struggle to defend deviations from the more traditional and pervasive models. Whenever a model moves away from prevailing practices, those using it can feel vulnerable to criticism and attack from more conservative practitioners. It is important for such pioneers to find support with others who are attempting to question the status quo. And of course it is important to be deliberate and thoughtful in introducing changes into clinical practice.

Because RCT therapy is driven by theory and philosophy rather than technique, it may pose special challenges for beginning students and for those who are teaching it. Careful supervision, with ample opportunity to discuss how one works with mutual empathy and authenticity, is particularly needed. Attention is paid to the importance of respect and thoughtful use of emotional responsiveness. Supervisors are called on to help students learn the difference between "letting it all hang out" ("amygdala authenticity") and finding the "one true thing" to share that will facilitate the movement of therapy. In RCT therapy supervision, students get to practice therapeutic authenticity and responsiveness, getting feedback from supervisors, who can assist in differentiating potentially helpful from less helpful "authentic" interventions. Supervision assists the beginning therapist in differentiating reactivity from responsiveness (Downs, 2006). RCT further emphasizes that the therapist's intention is to assist in the client's growth and healing; as a change agent, the therapist holds a great deal of responsibility for the well-being of the client, the relationship, and the work. There are no shortcuts to learning these differentiations. Therapists who have been trained in more traditional modes of therapy have to learn to work with mutuality and not to confuse it with reciprocity or lack of role differentiation. Furthermore, therapists must cultivate some comfort with uncertainty and an attitude of constant learning. Because relational–cultural therapy is based in maintaining a respectful attitude, developing relational awareness, and does not provide many technical guidelines, supervision for the beginner is especially important (Downs, 2006; Lenz, 2014; Pack, 2009).

The poet John Keats (1818/1987) once wrote about the importance of "staying in uncertainty, Mystery and doubt without irritable reaching after fact or reason." One practitioner (Roseann Adams, 2005, personal communication) rearranged the first letter of this to the acronym "MUD"— mystery, uncertainty, and doubt; we are invited to stay with the unclear, the inevitable messiness of human relationships. We live in a culture that presses for certainty, that equates competence with mastery. In this context, therapists must devote energy to staying connected through uncertainty and doubt. Sometimes we do not have a clear sense of what is going on; sometimes we are quite lost. In those moments, we continue our commitment to the relationship, and we may even join the client in her or his sense of helplessness in the moment. But by staying present and connected, we alter the experience of uncertainty. Sometimes we need to acknowledge how hard it is to stay in a place of not knowing in a culture that places such a premium on knowledge and certainty.

mystery / uncertainty / doubt

5

Evaluation

The growing body of relational–cultural theory (RCT) research will contribute to our understanding of how relationships heal and how broadly applicable these ideas are to various areas of academic inquiry and social action. The RCT and therapy research network serves as a resource for many researchers throughout the United States and the world who are interested in using this theory in their work. Since 1996, the Jean Baker Miller Training Institute has held an annual RCT research forum each spring. We now invite RCT poster sessions presented by practitioners at our intensive institute. RCT has been used in numerous dissertation projects and has also been represented increasingly in peer-reviewed journals, books, and book chapters (e.g., Armstrong, 2008; Comstock et al., 2008; Deanow, 2011; Englar-Carlson, Evans, & Duffey, 2014; Frager & Fadiman, 1998; Frey, 2013; Headley & Sangganjanavanich, 2014; Jordan,

http://dx.doi.org/10.1037/0000063-005
Relational–Cultural Therapy, Second Edition, by J. V. Jordan
Copyright © 2018 by the American Psychological Association. All rights reserved.

2008d; Liang, Tracy, Kenny, Brogan, & Gatha, 2010; Mereish & Poteat, 2015; Miller, 2008a, 2008b; M. Walker, 2008a, 2008b).

Practitioners and researchers alike have been investigating and expanding different aspects of the ever-evolving RCT. Comstock et al. (2008) provided an overview of the ways in which RCT bridges relational, multicultural, and social justice competencies. Eldridge, Surrey, Rosen, and Miller (2008) examined what changes in therapy. An entire volume of *Women & Therapy* (Jordan, 2008d) was devoted to documenting recent developments in RCT. Miller (2008a, 2008b) has elaborated on the role of power in relationships and in therapy. Stiver, Rosen, Surrey, and Miller (2008) examined the impact of cultural disconnections on the therapy relationship, noting that both client and therapist are "carriers" of cultural disconnections. Maureen Walker (2008a, 2008b) has pointed to the need for a new understanding of power, suggesting we see it as the energy of competence in everyday living. Jordan (2009) reflected on changes in RCT therapy and pointed to the need for an abiding curiosity toward what creates change in life and in therapy. Brubaker (2010) reviewed relational–cultural therapy and noted that it had gained prominence and acceptance with many practitioners; he named its core as the idea that interpersonal connection rather than independence is at the center of personal growth. In a special section of the October 2016 *Journal of Counseling & Development* (a volume that was in large part devoted to RCT), Lenz (2016) gave an overview of the empirical literature supporting RCT. He noted that RCT provides a useful framework for understanding client experiences and also found that there is considerable support for the psychometric validation of RCT constructs. He added, however, that support for RCT interventions is still limited. Strong psychometric properties of the Mutual Psychological Development Questionnaire (MPDQ), Relational Health Indices (RHI), and Connection–Disconnection Scale (CDS) suggest that the RCT constructs are well defined, leading to strong reliability and evidence of validity. RCT interventions also were seen to be helpful for both women and men experiencing eating disorders, depression, social skills deficits, and delinquency. More studies assessing efficacy across settings and client populations are needed, however.

Much of the research stimulated by RCT has focused on and affirmed the validity of its theoretical framework; this validity is also supported by studies coming from related fields. The burgeoning field of neuroscience has provided wide and convincing support for the core precepts of RCT: We are hardwired to connect; we suffer in isolation and exclusion; we need relationships like we need air and water; we thrive in growth-fostering relationships. Several studies have also specifically confirmed the efficacy of RCT therapy (Lenz, 2016; Oakley et al., 2013).

RESEARCH ON RCT PSYCHOTHERAPY OUTCOMES

Studies of RCT therapy outcomes have focused on specific interventions. In Oakley et al.'s 2013 study of the efficacy of RCT therapy, Anne Oakley, Shirley Addison, and members of the research team at the Brief Psychotherapy Centre for Women in Toronto conducted a 2-year outcome study funded by the Ontario Women's Health Council of the Ministry of Health of Ontario. Since the early 2000s, this group from a small community-based service has developed and practiced a brief model of therapy using RCT. Their research indicated that clients improved significantly on all eight outcome measures studied; gains were maintained at 6 and 9 months after the completion of RCT therapy (Oakley & Addison, 2005; Oakley et al., 2013). This is the first published study of the effectiveness of a brief relational–cultural model of therapy.

Lenz (2016) provided an extensive review of research on RCT, noting that "it is imperative to determine the present state of empirical literature that bolsters the utility of this approach to counselors" (p. 415). He looked at research articles published in counseling journals from 2000 to 2012 and reported on eight studies that support RCT as a framework for explaining experiences of clients (Beyene, Anglin, Sanchez, & Ballou, 2002; Kayser, Watson, L., & Andrade, 2007; Liang, Spencer, Brogan, & Corral, 2008; Spencer, 2006; Spencer, Jordan, & Sazama, 2004). A review of 27 studies supports the theoretical constructs of RCT. Eleven studies used the MPDQ to evaluate relationships between mutuality and emotional well-being and found that mutuality may be a good predictor of several outcomes in psychosocial domains (Auslander, Perfect, Succop, & Rosenthal, 2007; Gerlock, 2001, 2004; Sanftner, Ryan, & Pierce, 2009; Sanftner, Tantillo, & Seidlitz, 2004; Sanftner et al., 2006; Sormanti & Kayser, 2000; S. G. Turner, Kaplan, & Badger, 2006; S. G. Turner, Kaplan, Zayas, & Ross, 2002; E. K. Walker, 2011; Zayas, Bright, Alvarez-Sánchez, & Cabassa, 2009). Participation in RCT groups was associated with strong relationships with peers across gender (Liang, Tracy, Kenny, & Brogan, 2008).

ASSESSMENTS AND EVALUATIONS OF RCT

In Norcross, VandenBos, and Freedheim's (2010) *History of Psychotherapy: Continuity and Change*, RCT is seen as calling for a shift from the prevailing paradigm of "the separate self" in Western psychology to a paradigm of "being-in-relation" (Jordan, 2011b). West (2005) pointed out that psychological theory building has long been dominated by White European perspectives; she noted that RCT provides an elaboration of some of the most basic feminist principles. West recommended RCT highly for advanced undergraduate and graduate students. In reviewing therapeutic applications of RCT, Koss-Chioino (2007) noted that this "new theoretical model" has gained prominence and acceptance with many practitioners. The review concluded that relational–cultural therapy provides a solid basis for a graduate class introduction to the foundations of the field. Koss-Chioino (2007), in reviewing the *Complexity of Connection*, pointed to the "outstanding" work of the Stone Center. The group is described as one of, or perhaps the foremost, group developing feminist approaches to psychotherapy. In making culture the centerpiece and pointing to social and political values informing theory, it goes beyond being a feminist-only project. It also provides an analysis of the dynamics of power and the flow of mutual empathy. Freedberg (2007) reexamined empathy from a relational feminist point of view; she pointed out that, in line with the RCT view, empathy is increasingly conceptualized as mutual, interactive, and humanist. Duffey and Somody (2011) pointed to the strength-based, contextually focused, and wellness perspective of RCT.

Headley and Sangganjanavanich (2014) presented RCT interventions in a "how to" manner, outlining key concepts and structures. RCT's focus on the suffering caused by chronic disconnection and isolation and the effects of privilege, marginalization, and cultural forces is emphasized in the American Psychological Association's (APA's) primer *Psychotherapy Theories and Techniques: A Reader* (VandenBos, Meidenbauer, & Frank-McNeil, 2014). Sparks (2009) provided a personal account of how she learned to be authentic with clients. Questions of self-disclosure and "being real" are among the more important issues for RCT practitioners, especially for practitioners new to RCT. RCT represents *therapy in the interest of social justice* (Hoffnung, 2005); Comstock (2005) noted that core to the model is a critique of prevailing social arrangements. Cannon, Patton, and Reicherzer (2014) noted that RCT provides an important emphasis on power and privilege that is lacking in traditional psycho-dynamic approaches (see also Patton & Reicherzer, 2010). Comstock et al. (2008) pointed out that RCT provides a framework for bridging relational, multicultural, and social justice competencies. In particular, they noted that through this framework, mental health professionals can explore how issues related to sex-role socialization, power, dominance, marginalization, and subordination affect the mental health and relational development of all people. Duffey and Haberstroh (2012) further explored the ways that RCT provides an integrative framework that helps clients develop personal awareness and relational functioning. Using RCT, Edwards, Gomes, and Major (2013) looked at the economic environment and its impact on parental psychological distress and the development of children, adolescents, and young adults. They called for policymakers and practitioners to collaborate in developing support strategies to sustain vulnerable populations. Economic and power-imbalance stressors are accorded significant importance in relational–cultural practice. Economic inequality erodes empathy, and marginalization created by power differences leads to isolation and disempowerment.

Frey, Tobin, and Beesley (2004) looked at the relational predictors of psychological distress in women and men presenting for university counseling center services. Frey (2013) reviewed RCT research and its application to counseling competencies and suggested that teaching RCT can play a role in building counseling skills among counseling students. In her overview of RCT, Frey included research that provided support regarding its assumptions, practice applications, and effectiveness. She concluded that RCT can provide an organized systematic structure for the development of therapeutic relationship-building skills and a framework for examining issues of power, privilege, oppression, and marginalization.

RESEARCH ON RCT THEORETICAL MODELS

Mutuality

Although mutuality is an important relational dimension, few researchers have examined the specific elements that contribute to mutuality. *Mutuality* involves "openness to influence, emotional availability, and a constantly changing pattern of responding to and affecting the other's state" (Jordan, 1986, p. 1). Genero, Miller, Surrey, and Baldwin (1992) developed the MPDQ, a 22-item self-report scale that measures perceived mutuality with partners and friends in a college-community sample of women. The MPDQ is designed to be a dyadic questionnaire that considers both the perspective of the respondent and the "target person"; completed by the respondent, it encompasses his or her perception of both sides of the relationship. The scale has been used extensively in work on the treatment of eating disorders, where it has confirmed the relevance of mutuality to positive treatment outcomes (Sanftner & Tantillo, 2001; Sanftner et al., 2006; Sanftner, Tantillo, & Seidlitz, 2004). In a clinical case study of therapist self-disclosure, Tantillo (2004) found that using RCT notions of mutuality in therapy validated clients, promoted empathy, fostered a sense of universality, reinforced the normalcy of the patient experiences, and conveyed flexibility and openness to change and difference.

Relational Health Indices

Derived from the RCT definition of growth-fostering relationships, Liang and colleagues (Land, Chan, & Liang, 2014; Liang et al., 1998; Liang, Tracy, Taylor, & Williams, 2002) developed the RHI to assess growth-fostering connections with peers, mentors, and communities. This 37-item measure assesses three conceptual dimensions of growth-fostering relationships:

engagement, authenticity, and empowerment/zest. The RHI components generally demonstrated good overall internal consistency. The scale provides a way to understand important, subtle qualities of complex dynamics of dyadic and group relationships, especially among women. Relational health, as measured by the RHI, was generally associated with mental health and adjustment in college-age women. Growth-fostering community relationships were likely to be associated with decreased stress and depression, suggesting that a sense of belonging not just in dyadic relationships but also in a larger community offers positive mental health benefits (Liang, Tracy, Taylor, & Williams, 2002; Liang, Tracy, Taylor, Williams, Jordan, & Miller, 2002; Maley, 2007). Liang, Tracy, Glenn, Burns, and Ting (2007) further explored the use of RHI with men by examining the generalizability of the measure's factor structure and convergent validity in males. They found significant validation of the use of the measure for men as well as women. Recently Liang and her colleagues have been developing a scale for use with children. The RHI has been adapted and used to assess perceived mutuality with mothers and fathers (Tantillo & Sanftner, 2003). Liang, the leading scholar in developing the original RHI (Liang et al., 1998), has continued to expand the application of the RHI to boys and men, Asian American populations, and European college students. Liang et al. (2010) adapted the RHI for youth (RHI–Y) to study growth-fostering relationships among early and mid-adolescents They developed a six-item scale assessing relational health in three relationship domains: friendship, relationship with an adult mentor, and relationship with members of a community group. Liang et al. (2010) also examined gender differences in the relational health of youth participating in social competency programs. Liang and West (2011) studied the relationship between relational health and alexithymia. Frey, Beesley, and Miller (2006) examined relational health, parental attachment, and psychological distress in college men and women. Liang et al. (2006) looked at the relationship between depression and relational health in Asian American and European American College women. LaBrie et al. (2008) found that strong relational health is associated with fewer negative alcohol-related consequences.

Eight sets of authors found the RHI were positively associated with resilience (Belford, Kaehler, & Birrell, 2012; Frey et al., 2004, 2006; Gibson

& Myers, 2002; LaBrie et al., 2008; Liang, Tracy, Taylor, & Williams, 2002; Liang & West, 2011; Liang, Williams, & Siegel, 2006). Four studies indicated a strong negative relationship among relational health variables, psychological distress, and trauma (Frey et al., 2006; Gibson & Myers, 2002; Liang, Tracy, Taylor, & Williams, 2002; Liang & West, 2011). Higher levels of relational health are associated with fewer negative effects related to traumatic events.

Connection–Disconnection Scale

Tantillo and Sanftner (2010a) developed and tested the CDS to increase understanding about the role of relational mutuality in eating disorders. In evaluating the psychometric properties associated with the CDS, they found strong test–retest reliability and internal consistency for the construct of perceived mutuality (Tantillo & Sanftner, 2010b). The CDS is a 16-item, self-report inventory constructed to measure eight RCT values that describe growth-fostering relationships: authenticity, engagement, empowerment, zest, respect for diversity, increased self-worth, and desire for more connection.

In CDS research related to disordered eating, Tantillo and Sanftner (2003) found that a 16-week RCT intervention was equivalent in efficacy to cognitive behavior therapy for decreasing symptoms associated with eating disorders. Their research also showed that low levels of perceived mutuality with others was significantly associated with high levels of bulimia and depressive symptoms. RCT-based interventions have also been shown to be effective in promoting positive relational change (authenticity, empowerment, engagement, and empathy) among incarcerated adolescent girls (Lenz, Speciale, & Aguilar, 2012).

RCT constructs are strong predictors for criterion variables associated with trauma, substance use, and symptoms related to eating disorders. RCT offers an alternative to the medical model for conceptualizing contributing factors to different problems. Although more randomized studies between groups are needed, these studies indicate RCT interventions and ways of framing problems may be helpful for both women and men, particularly for those with eating disorders, depression, social skills deficits, and delinquency.

The studies described in the preceding sections offer moderate to strong support for the use of RCT constructs. The strong psychometric properties of the MPDQ, RHI, and CDS indicate that RCT constructs are well defined in a manner that has yielded evidence of solid reliability and validity (Lenz et al., 2012). Lenz and colleagues (2012) stated that these instruments can be used as the foundation for assessment- and evidence-based treatment planning.

Mentoring

Research on mentoring has also made use of RCT constructs. In a study of mentoring college-age women using a relational approach, Liang, Tracy, Kauh, Taylor, and Williams (2006) found that the presence of relational qualities in the mentoring relationship (e.g., empathy, engagement, authenticity, empowerment) strongly influences the success of mentoring in the lives of young women. They found that mentoring relationships high in relational qualities were associated with higher self-esteem and less loneliness. Spencer (2006; Spencer, Jordan, & Sazama, 2004) found that adolescents place a high value on respect, mutuality, and authenticity in their relationships with adults. An examination of the relationships between young men and adult male mentors indicated that finding a safe place for vulnerability and emotional support was an important aspect of these relationships (Spencer, 2007); this was also found to be true in relationships between adolescent girls and adult women in formal youth mentoring relationships (Spencer & Liang, 2009). Another study suggests that mentoring programs need to find a way to promote authentic exchange within relationships between young men and their adult mentors (Spencer, 2006). Empathy has also been found to be an essential aspect of more successful mentoring relationships (Larsson, Pettersson, Skoog, & Eriksson, 2016; Schwartz, 2010).

Schwartz and Holloway (2012) studied mentoring in graduate education and found that meaningful interactions with faculty can help graduate students progress through their academic work. McMillan-Roberts (2015) examined the impact of mutuality on doctoral students and faculty mentoring relationships and found that mutuality enhanced the working relationship. Several other researchers have also used RCT in their mentoring research: Munson, Smalling, Spencer, Scott, and Tracy (2010) conducted thematic analyses informed by RCT to explore the nature of nonkin natural mentors in the lives of youth; Schwartz and Holloway (2014) emphasized the importance of a mutuality-informed mentoring program for graduate students; and A. R. Alvarez and Lazzari (2016) noted that feminists who often find themselves isolated in the academy can benefit from feminist mentoring. RCT emphasizes the value of mutual learning in mentoring relationships where both participants are open to being changed by their interactions. Role differences are respected, but the idea of one "power over" teacher and one recipient learner (mentee) is questioned. Where growth-fostering relationships are pursued, both people participate in learning and in contributing to the well-being of the other (McMillan, 2011).

Humiliation Studies

Humiliation is a destructive form of disconnection—a profound relational violation—that has recently gained the attention of a growing number of scholars and research scientists around the world. Using RCT as a theoretical foundation, Linda Hartling (1995; Hartling & Lindner, 2016; Hartling & Luchetta, 1999) developed the first scale designed to assess the impact of humiliation in various forms, including social exclusion, ridicule, devaluation, and denigration. Items from this scale are being incorporated into a multidimensional survey of poverty being developed by Sabina Alkire at the Oxford Poverty and Human Development Initiative, University of Oxford in England (Sabina Alkire, personal communication to L. M. Hartling, December 6, 2007). One goal of this survey is to give rise to internationally comparable data examining economic hardship and the intensity of shame and humiliation. According to Alkire, items from the humiliation scale tested well in the Gallup Poll in Bolivia, so they are extending their study to nine other nations. Edwards, Gomes, and Major (2013) found that RCT can be useful in understanding the impact of the economy on vulnerable populations. In particular, they called for policymakers and practitioners to facilitate support strategies among adolescents and young adults.

Patients With Cancer

RCT has been applied to women coping with cancer in a series of studies by Kayser, Sormanti, and Strainchamps (1999). In these studies, relational coping was initially conceptualized as women's coping abilities that are shaped by and continue to develop in the context of close relationships. Relational factors such as mutuality were found to have a significant influence on the women's adjustment to cancer. Specifically, mutuality was significantly related to a higher level of quality of life and self-care agency and had a significant negative relationship with depression. A follow-up study with these women 2 years later found the same strong relationships between mutuality and women's adjustment to cancer (Kayser & Sormanti, 2002a). A common theme in these research studies was the women's rethinking the balance of self-care and other-care (Kayser & Sormanti, 2002a). Thus, women's concerns about how to maintain connections with friends and family members during illness may need to be addressed in the assessment and treatment phases, a factor often left out of treatment planning.

The concept of relational coping was further expanded and applied to couples coping with cancer. Whereas earlier work conceptualized a woman's coping within the relational context, Kayser's more recent research (Kayser, 2005; Kayser & Sormanti, 2002b) has focused on how the couple copes together when facing a common stressor—that is, how the coping is conceptualized as a dyadic or interactive phenomenon. Two distinct patterns of relational coping were identified in a study of couples coping with breast cancer: mutual responsiveness and disengaged avoidance. The relational qualities of relationship awareness, authenticity, and mutuality played a pivotal role in the type of pattern of coping that the couples demonstrated (Kayser, Watson, & Andrade, 2007). Kayser and Scott (2008) published a treatment protocol for working with couples facing a woman's cancer. This couple-based approach builds on couples' strengths, transforming a potentially painful experience into one in which each person grows through the connection with the other. Additional recent research by Kayser and her colleagues has focused on the sociocultural factors that influence a couple's coping patterns. These studies by Kayser (2007) and Kayser and coworkers (2014) examined the influence of culture on couples coping with breast cancer. The authors provided a comparative analysis of couples from China, India, and the United States, and their research revealed several cultural factors that may influence the process of coping with breast cancer, including family boundaries, gender roles, personal control, and interdependence. Additionally, Johannessen (2013) found that cancer patients consistently identify their relationships as "meaning the most" to them. Bekteshi and Kayser (2013) examined mothers' perceptions of the effects their cancer experience had on their relationships with daughters, focusing on emotional connection or disconnection. Most reported closer relationships with their daughters. As these studies illustrate, the relational context is central to healing and largely determines the quality of life of patients with cancer.

Parenting

An intervention program with new mothers referred for isolation, anxiety about parenting, lack of support or limited resources, and postpartum depression demonstrates another application of RCT (Dubus, 2014; Paris, Gemborys, Kaufman, & Whitehill, 2007). Conducted by volunteer home visitors, the program has a specific relational perspective that has provided coherence to the screening, training, and supervision of volunteers. RCT in particular helps the volunteers in their work with the new mother. Mutuality and authenticity were hallmarks of the home visiting relationships. A qualitative study of 15 at-risk mothers visited by volunteers suggests that validation, affirmation, consistency, and emotional and instrumental aid were important to the new mothers. Their self-confidence in caring for their babies increased, and they also sought more interpersonal connection. Most new mothers were surprised at how lonely and disconnected they felt. The relationships with the home visitors were described in over-whelmingly positive terms. Most felt more competent as mothers—more connected, empowered, and taken care of—as a result of the intervention. This study specifically points to the usefulness of volunteer, paraprofessional, home-visiting interventions based on a relational model. This could serve as a template for other community agencies (Paris & Dubus, 2005; Paris, Gemborys, Kaufman, & Whitehill, 2007).

In examining difficult relationships between adult children and parents, some authors have suggested these relationships can become "poisonous" or "toxic." RCT prefers to bring awareness to the patterns of disconnection and look at possible ways to address chronic disconnection (Jordan, 2011a). Emphasizing the cultural and societal factors that affect parenting (racism, sexism, shame, classism, unrealistic expectations for primary caregivers), RCT calls for a more compassionate understanding of flawed parent–child relationships. Clearly, there are occasions when parents are destructive, and we do not mean to ignore those; when relationships are abusive or chronically undermining, they are not healthy, and children should be protected. But too often parents are blamed and pathologized when we could more usefully seek understanding of the challenges that most parents face and provide support and education aimed at developing more relationally competent interactions. Jordan (2011a) looked at the parent–child relationship in its social context, validating the pain created by social forces such as racism, sexism, and shaming; she validated the difficulty of the job of mothering or parenting in a context that offers inadequate support for caregivers. Too often research on parenting limits its analysis to the parent–child dyad or the nuclear family, overlooking the pervasive stress created in a "go it alone" culture. Paris and Dubus (2005) addressed the challenges for mothers to stay connected with support systems while nurturing an infant.

RCT research has also been conducted to better understand relational development in individuals: Deanow (2011) proposed a model of development that highlights relational developmental tasks and obstacles throughout the life cycle rather than looking for markers of autonomy and independence; Etienne (2011) studied African American mother–daughter relationships using an RCT lens; Melles and Frey (2014) used

RCT to understand adult third-culture kids; and Beesley and Frey (2008) used RCT in group work promoting social and emotional competence among students, counselors, teachers, parents, and administration.

RELATED RESEARCH

The APA has attempted to identify empirically supported treatments (ESTs) for adults. Norcross (2002) pointed out that "the therapist as a person is a central agent of change. . . . both clinical experience and research findings underscore that the therapy relationship accounts for as much of the outcome variance as particular treatments" (p. 5). Norcross emphasized the importance of identifying empirically supported therapy relationships rather than empirically supported treatments (ESRs rather than ESTs). An APA Division 29 (Psychotherapy) Task Force undertook this project (Norcross, 2002). Task force participants proposed that both treatment approaches and relationship variables contribute to outcome in therapy.

In related non–RCT-based research on the importance of connection, Resnick and colleagues (1997) found in a study of 12,000 adolescents that a strong emotional connection with one adult reduces the odds that an adolescent will experience emotional stress, have suicidal thoughts or behavior, engage in violence, or abuse alcohol or other drugs.

Shelly Taylor, an expert in stress research at UCLA, noted that almost all studies of the classic fight-or-flight response to stress were done on male organisms (male rats, male macaque monkeys, and men; Taylor, 2002; Taylor et al., 2000). When Taylor and colleagues replicated these studies of stress using females, they found that females had a different response, something they called the "tend-and-befriend" response. Under stress, females tended to turn to others to (depending on species) groom, huddle, or talk. In part this seems to be related to the release of oxytocin in the female brain in stressful situations. This hormone is sometimes called the "affiliative hormone" because it is associated with seeking proximity and reduction of social anxiety. This study supported the need for gender analysis in the study of stress and also pointed to the importance of connecting with others, particularly for females who are stressed.

NEUROSCIENCE FINDINGS

The brain is composed of about 100 billion interconnected neurons. At birth the brain is the most undifferentiated organ in the body. One of the most powerful and critical influences on brain development and functioning is relationships. In particular, the orbitofrontal cortex (OFC), the part of the brain responsible for early connection with caregivers, goes through a lot of pruning in the first 3 years of life. The brain is programmed to learn and programmed to make connections, internally between neurons and externally with a responsive caregiver. New information about brain development explodes the myth of one-way influence (from mother to baby). We now know that the brain activity of the mother directly influences the brain activity of the baby and vice versa (Schore, 1994). Each person is influencing and being influenced by the other; in empathic exchange, both are positively affected by the responsive cascade–release of chemicals in each of their brains. The path of development is a path of mutuality and responsiveness. Eye contact, facial expression, and voice tone all contribute to emotional and neurological resonance (Goleman, 2006). Mutual gaze increases the levels of monoamine neurotransmitters in mother and child. Caregiver and baby, in mutual gaze, are entranced, interacting, opening to greater energy, sliding away from one another, then back toward one another, joining in a dance of attunement, a dance sculpting the prefrontal cortex, right hemisphere to right hemisphere. Physical touch, holding, and hugs stimulate neurotransmitter release. Brain growth and shaping also continue way beyond the early, intense interactions between baby and caregiver.

Eisenberger and Lieberman (2005) noted that social pain, exclusion, and the anticipation of exclusion register in the same area of the brain as physical pain, the anterior cingulate cortex (ACC). The ACC has the highest density of opioid receptors in the entire central nervous system; opioids are released upon social contact, decreasing both physical and social pain. The body and its nervous system hold the truth: We need relationships. Social relationships are like air and water. We need them to live. We feel pain when we are blocked from them. Babies who are physically well cared for but given no social interaction die. In the past, social scientists suggested that relationships were important only because a caregiver was associated with the cessation of a primary drive; for example, the mother's face was linked with being nursed or fed. The need for relationships was never seen as a primary motivation in its own right. RCT posits that we need social connection throughout the lifespan, and neurological research is supporting this claim (Eisenberger & Lieberman, 2005).

To be disconnected creates pain, and social pain is *real* pain. Eisenberger and Lieberman (2005) determined that the social pain of exclusion and even the anticipation of social exclusion, follow the same neural pathways and register in the same area of the brain as the pain created by physical injury. Beyond the implications for an individual's pain secondary to loss of relationship or even the anticipation of loss of relationship, this supports RCT's contention that marginalization, rejection, and social isolation create enormous pain. Often in our culture, psychological or emotional suffering is seen as less real or compelling than physical pain. It is dismissed as "all in your head." Thus, if we are fearful of being separated from those we love or feel the terrible pain of being rejected by a group of friends or peers, we are often treated as being "too needy" or too "soft," as wimps. It is a part of the stiff-upper-lip mentality that suggests we are "better" people if we can "suck it up," grin and bear it, and definitely stifle tears. This code applies especially harshly to males (Lombardi, 2011; Pollack, 1998). The lack of appreciation of social pain allows us to minimize the pain of social prejudice, oppression, and bullying. Eisenberger and Lieberman (2005) suggested that "the pain mechanisms involved in preventing physical danger were co-opted to prevent social separation" (p. 4). Our brains are programmed to avoid not only the pain of physical injury but interpersonal hurt and social isolation as well. Connection is so essential to human life that our brains are wired to respond to the threat of exclusion or isolation in the same way we are wired to respond to life-threatening injury or lack of air or water. Connection is crucial to our existence. We do not simply need to attach to nurturing others as infants and children; we need to be in growth-fostering relationships throughout our entire lives.

This study (Eisenberger & Lieberman, 2005) has important implications for the understanding of individual suffering from isolation or exclusion. Without connection, a sense of being included, our well-being is endangered. But the study also has profound social implications. It tells us that people who are marginalized, excluded, or left out suffer real pain. It thus invites an appreciation that the pain of racism, homophobia, sexism, and all forms of social marginalization is real; racism, heterosexism, and classism not only silence and disempower, they also create real pain, which has a destructive impact on individuals. This finding supports the social justice implications of RCT. RCT posits that human beings are basically oriented toward connection and points out the ways that stratifying social structures create chronic isolation and disempowerment for many people. Taking seriously the evidence of the pain of exclusion and marginalization and challenging the dominant paradigm of separation constitute action toward social justice. A sociopolitical system based on the intrinsic worth of mutually respectful relationships would indeed be a system that translates into a more just society. Although most theories do not extend the psychological paradigm to the sociopolitical realm, RCT does so explicitly. Building on observations of the relational development of individual brains, along with theories about the impact of dyadic interactions on the brain, it points to the social implications of these observations.

The growth of the OFC depends on the attunement of parents. If parents are unresponsive or abusive, the child is left with a deficit in the ability to regulate the length, intensity, or frequency of distressing emotions such as anger, terror, or shame. Siegel (1999) noted that when in empathic attunement, the brains of both mother and infant are changing. Schore (1994) demonstrated that growth of the OFC depends on relational experience. Goleman (2006), in reviewing Schore's work, noted that the neural site for emotional malfunction is the OFC. Although both Schore and Siegel have argued for the importance of early nurturing relationships in shaping the brain, they both have also stated that nurturing relationships—what RCT practitioners refer to as *growth-fostering relationships*—later in life can rework some of these neural pathways. RCT argues this neural and relational repair occurs with great intensity in relational psychotherapy.

With the new data on neuroplasticity, we are learning how interactions reshape our brain (Begley, 2008; Doidge, 2007; Merzenich, 2000).

The shape, size, and number of neurons and their synaptic connections are sculpted by relationships. This leads to the optimistic position that growth-fostering relationships later in life can, to some extent, rework old, destructive neural patterns.

When RCT was first being constructed as a developmental and clinical model, it was greeted with great skepticism, even alarm, by many traditional practitioners. The suggestion that there be more therapeutic transparency was seen as a challenge to the rather widespread practice of therapist opaqueness—at its extreme, the "blank screen." Although many in the field saw the fallacy of the effectiveness of such an approach, others clung to it as essential to "cure" and feared that something like mutual empathy would result in clients feeling they had to "take care of the therapist." The importance of the client's seeing her or his impact on others, learning new ways of being in relationship, and feeling that she or he "matters" was not appreciated. For those in particular who live in invalidating or abusive relationships, responsiveness from the therapist is important in establishing a sense of safety. For the abuse survivor, entering a relationship with a powerful other, behind closed doors where their vulnerability is supposedly protected, signals alarm rather than comfort. RCT puts forth the idea of reworking neuronal pathways and relational images by creating new relational experiences; at the same time, the client gains a perspective on the context in which the original expectations were laid down and makes new meaning of these images. Current, cutting-edge neuroscience research provides strong support for the notion of neuroplasticity through relational engagement, points to the intrinsic movement toward mutual relationship, and validates the efficacy of the RCT model.

6

Future Developments

It is now more than 40 years since the inception of relational–cultural theory (RCT), and its primary use has been in long-term individual therapy. But practitioners offering different approaches have also applied RCT to their work. What follows is a summary of some of these newer practices with suggestions for how RCT will be developed in the future.

RCT is based on knowledge that growth occurs in relationships and that we are hardwired for empathic attunement and belonging. If we are excluded or socially isolated, we experience significant pain. We need relationships like we need air and water. Mutual empathy is at the core of building growth-fostering relationships. If we support personal growth characterized by mutual empathy, we are essentially supporting the development of respect and investment in growth for all people in the relationship. This runs counter to the dominant narrative of individual

http://dx.doi.org/10.1037/0000063-006
Relational–Cultural Therapy, Second Edition, by J. V. Jordan

competition and establishing dominance over others (Jordan, 2008a, 2008b, 2008c, 2008d). In line with the emphasis on social ramifications of RCT, Jordan addressed the importance of new definitions of courage, built in a context of "supported vulnerability." She noted that in a culture of fear, connections serve as an antidote to fear and a sense of powerlessness. Jordan (2008a, 2008b, 2008c, 2008d) has also pointed to the need for new models of "strength." Noting that marginalization actively disempowers and wounds people, Jordan proposed a model of "strength in supported vulnerability," an alternative to strength in isolation and standing strong alone.

THERAPEUTIC MILIEUS AND TOOLS

Couples Therapy

RCT therapy has been used in working with couples, both individually and in groups. In their relational approach, Bergman and Surrey (1994, 2013) have addressed the importance of the *we* rather than the *I*. They often begin their group work by asking couples to introduce "the relationship" rather than each individual. Couples are also encouraged to write a relational purpose statement. The core relational principles guiding couples therapy include holding relational awareness, working toward mutually empathic connection, taking mutual responsibility, and working with gender issues. The concept of mutual impact becomes helpful for moving out of the power and control struggles that plague many couples. RCT also brings awareness to the crucial impact of context and power arrangements on couples (Eldridge, 2013; Mirkin & Geib, 2013; M. Walker, 2013). Knudson-Martin et al. (2015) drew on the work of RCT to introduce socioemotional therapy, which looks at the emotional distress caused by power and gender imbalances within relationships. Besides therapy, RCT has been used to better understand the power of relationships and to develop a framework for holding awareness of self, other, and the relationship (Shem & Surrey, 1998; Skerrett, 2016; Skerrett & Fergus, 2015). S. Johnson's (2008) work on the importance of attachment styles in working with couples also has much in common with RCT therapy.

Jordan and Carlson (2013) edited *Creating Connection: A Relational-Cultural Approach With Couples*, which included a chapter interviewing Bergman and Surrey, who did much of the early work with the application of RCT to couples therapy (Bergman & Surrey, 2013); other chapters focused on working with same-sex couples (Eldridge, 2013; Shannon, 2013), dynamics of mixed-race couples (M. Walker, 2013), naming the work of motherhood (Malik, 2013), the impact of context on couples (Mirkin & Geib, 2013), resilience in couples (Skerrett, 2013), helping remarried couples deal with the complex relationships with stepchildren (Lerner, 2013), a neurobiological–relational approach to couple therapy (Fishbane, 2013), evolving sexualities (Striepe, 2013), the challenges of divorce (Comstock-Benzick, 2013), special issues for men in heterosexual couples therapy (Markey, 2013), and working with couples facing health challenges (Johannessen, 2013). Kayser et al. (2014) have also done research on RCT and couples coping with breast cancer.

Family Therapy

Mirkin (1990, 1998) used RCT therapy in work with families and couples. She noted that when couples are having problems, the rupture in the relationship is often embedded in some larger contextual issue, which could include overall family dynamics (Mirkin & Geib, 1999). Once the issue is identified and named, the partners often regain their empathy and connection. Mirkin (1998) also looked at reframing disconnects between immigrant parents and children as being about acculturation and not simply personal battles. In families with adolescents, she has noted that avoidance of conflict may rupture relationships as much as or more than the conflict itself. The goal of adolescence with regard to families, she has suggested, is to develop age-appropriate connection rather than separation (Mirkin, 1990, 1992). In this regard, E. Carter and McGoldrick's (2005) "self in context" has much in common with RCT's earlier use of "self-in-relation" and "relational-being."

Group Therapy

As a culture we have become increasingly aware of the power of groups to help initiate and sustain personal and cultural change. Twelve-step programs have transformed our understanding and treatment of most addictions. As noted in an earlier chapter, RCT views 12-step programs as mutual help programs rather than self-help programs; healing occurs as one receives help from others but also as one provides understanding and care to others. RCT emphasizes the interdependent, mutual nature of healing—the need to connect and to engage in growth-fostering, caring relationships. In RCT group therapy, as in any kind of RCT therapy, "the ongoing dialectic between the desire for genuine, responsive and gratifying connections and the need to maintain strategies to stay out of connection is the pivotal experience" (Fedele, 2004, p. 202). The central relational paradox of honoring the yearning for connection and the protective movement into disconnection plays out in the tensions between wanting to be known, understood, and accepted, and the fears, so evident in a group, that one will not find empathy or acceptance. A group offers ample opportunity for working on acute disconnections; this builds relational resilience. As members respond empathically with other members, they often find new places of empathy for their own experience.

Psychoeducational Groups

RCT has also been used in time-limited psychoeducational groups. An eight-session program has been developed that includes both educational discussion groups and work on relational awareness (Jordan & Dooley, 2000). It introduces participants to the core processes of RCT through didactic and experiential means. This format has been used successfully in a wide variety of settings, including groups for inmates and guards at a women's prison, an inpatient trauma treatment unit, a community program for chronically psychotic patients, a group for 10- to 12-year-old boys, halfway houses, a group of Navajo adolescents, groups of girls in a Department of Youth Services residential program, and the staff of a partial hospitalization program. In addition to providing a suggested structure and readings for each of the eight sessions, the program elucidates the core concepts of RCT and provides handouts for participants.

Relational–Cultural Mindfulness

RCT therapy is not anchored in techniques or tools. Rather, it suggests that working with relationships (the therapeutic relationship as well as other relationships) is the central skill. Nonetheless, there are some tools that can be of use to this process. Because the success of RCT therapy depends heavily on the *quality of presence* of the therapist, the therapist must put significant effort into finding ways to engage *responsively* and not *reactively*. Mindfulness practices can be extremely beneficial for the relational–cultural therapist. Relational–cultural mindfulness is a particular kind of mindfulness that suggests we not only extend our awareness and attunement to the passing parade of images and thoughts in our minds and feelings in our bodies but that we also bring the meditational attitude of presence to our relational worlds. Particularly in a culture that is replete with messages of self-interest and looking at the self, there needs to be an emphasis on bringing attention to the relational world and one's community (Jordan, 1995a, 1995b; Surrey, 2005; Surrey & Eldridge, 2007; Surrey & Jordan, 2013).

Specifically, mindfulness meditation can be an important interpersonal tool for both therapist and client. More and more data are accumulating about the usefulness of meditation in treating depression, anxiety, and many other psychological conditions (Begley, 2008; Goleman, 2006; Williams, Teasdale, Segal, & Kabat-Zinn, 2007), and the data are mounting that meditation creates brain change (Begley, 2008). Therefore, the adjunctive practice of meditation is recommended for many clients. RCT would also suggest that the therapist's effectiveness could be improved by meditation. A study in Germany looked at outcome variables on 124 inpatients who were treated for 9 weeks by 18 therapists in training. The patients of therapists who meditated had significantly higher evaluations on two scales: clarification and problem-solving perspectives. Their evaluations were also significantly higher for the total therapeutic result, and they showed greater symptom reduction (Grepmair et al., 2007). Both Jordan and Surrey (of the original RCT group) studied with Vimala Thakar, a meditation teacher who worked with Krishnamurti. A social activist in India, she taught meditation/awareness practice in the West. One of her key insights was "To live is to be related" (V. Thakar, personal communication, 1991). In 2009, Jordan served on a panel at the Harvard Medical School on wisdom and compassion with the Dalai Lama and several experts on meditation and brain function. Since then, there has been a burgeoning interest in the convergent insights of neuroscience, mindfulness, and the primacy of connection in people's lives.

Jordan also presented in a program with Thich Nhat Hanh at the Harvard Medical School Conference "Meditation and Psychotherapy: Deepening Mindfulness" (September 11–12, 2013). Mindfulness and relational–cultural therapy share a worldview that emphasizes compassion, presence, nonjudgmental listening, connectedness, and moving beyond the constraints of the separate self. Mindfulness practice allows us to come more fully into relationship with what is: By being present and aware, we invite one another into the vulnerability of mutual change and growth. We create steady awareness when we sit in formal meditation, and we practice compassionate engagement when we bring that intention into our everyday lives and relationships.

Auxiliary Approaches

Medication can play an important role in many treatments. Where the client's reactivity or extreme negative relational images make it impossible for the client to even sit in the room to engage in therapy, medication can bring the person to a place of being able to entertain the possibility of engaging in the therapeutic relationship. Often with clients with posttraumatic stress disorder (PTSD), medication is a necessary intervention to bring about neurobiological quieting so that new learning can occur and new relational patterns can begin to form (Banks, 2005; Trepal, 2010; van der Kolk, 1988). Many RCT therapists also make use of cognitive behavioral approaches, particularly in helping people manage symptoms that may interfere with making connections. Many have used dialectical behavior therapy or eye movement desensitization reprocessing in working with trauma, and some have found internal family systems or narrative family therapy to be quite compatible with RCT therapy.

SPECIAL ISSUES AND POPULATIONS

Race and Marginalization

RCT has specifically addressed the pain and disconnection that arise as a result of stratification and marginalization along racial lines (Edwards, Bryant, & Clark, 2008; M. Walker, 2008a). Cholewa, Goodman, West-Olatunji, and Amatea (2014) conducted a qualitative examination of the impact of culturally responsive educational practices on the psychological well-being of students of color. Using culturally responsive education (CRE) practices, these authors noted that an environment can be created in which marginalized students thrive not only academically but psychologically. Liang, Tracy, Kauh, Taylor, and Williams (2006) studied the relationship between depression and relational health in Asian American and European American College women. M. Walker (2008a) wrote about the impact of culture and marginalization on the therapy process. Comstock (2005) examined how diversity and context are integral to any understanding of personal development and pathology. Edwards et al. (2008) applied RCT concepts to the experience of African American social work educators in predominantly white schools of social work. Using RCT principles, Packnett (2010) developed a retention plan for African American students who attend predominantly White institutions.

Using RCT's emphasis on the positive power of connection and the destructive power of isolation, a number of researchers have turned to RCT to help elucidate the dynamics of marginalization, exclusion, stratification, and "power over." Shibusawa and Chung (2009) studied RCT practice with East Asian immigrant elders. Moore (2011) looked at friendships between Black women and White women and suggested the importance of actively fostering connection in a culture of disconnection. Moore found that mutual empathic awareness and a willingness to deal with difference and conflict are essential to these relationships. Rassiger (2010) studied student–teacher relationships and academic success in an at-risk Latino and Black middle school, noting sizable gaps between low-income Latino and Black students and White middle-class students; Rassiger found that perceived teacher caring was predictive of academic success. Ruiz (2012) used RCT to better understand Latina immigrants, finding that they are at increased risk for major disconnection.

Another population that is negatively affected by marginalization and the isolation it produces is the LGBTQ community. Mainstream culture assumes and privileges heterosexuality, leaving nonheterosexual people at increased risk for disconnection and isolation. Nonmutuality may be an underlying requirement for the maintenance of sexism, racism, and heterosexism. These attitudes are characterized by a lack of empathy and resistance to mutual impact (Heineman, 2003). As Laing (1998) said, "Isolation is the glue that holds oppression in place." Isolation and chronic disconnection contribute significantly to disempowerment, depression, and anxiety.

PTSD

RCT therapy is particularly suited to working with clients with PTSD (Banks, 2000, 2006b). In many ways posttraumatic stress disorders are disorders of connection and isolation. People who have been traumatized have lived in unsafe, non–growth-fostering relationships. They have had to develop protective strategies of survival that often involve being split off from their real experience and rarely feeling safe enough to bring their vulnerability into relationship. People who have been traumatized suffer from immobilization, self-blame, isolation, and shame. Healing trauma involves bringing a person back into connection (Herman, 1992; Root, 1992). A history of trauma, particularly childhood sexual or physical abuse predisposes clients to a great deal of fear, even terror, which can be triggered by the therapy situation itself: Being invited into vulnerability behind dosed doors with another, more powerful person whom you are told you can trust is a powerful trigger for a victim of childhood abuse.

It is no wonder that the early weeks and months of therapy with clients with PTSD can be filled with abrupt disconnections, intense affect, and even self-destructive actions. For a trauma survivor, moving into more vulnerability with another person intensifies fear and reactivity (Banks, 2005; Herman, 1992; Root, 1992). Their strategies of disconnection—in these cases, traumatic disconnection—are heightened, and hypervigilance leads to frequent ruptures and amplified reactions. What might seem like "ordinary expectable empathic failures" in other therapies may be experienced by the client as life-threatening events or indications of the therapist's complete and total untrustworthiness. Their reactivity may even lead to the sense that the therapist is dangerous and predatory. The overly reactive amygdala often leads to exaggerated responses (Banks, 2005; van der Kolk, 1988). The reactive neurochemistry goes into emergency mode, and abrupt retreat into further isolation often occurs. Ironically, these traumatic disconnections can occur when there is an empathic failure on the part of the therapist but also when there is increasing connection. The latter occurs as the client begins to relinquish strategies for disconnection (by coming close and being more authentic and hence more vulnerable), and then panic sets in and the client overreacts to an increased sense of vulnerability with a major disconnection. The therapist, who may feel bewildered by this sudden turn, must try to stay present, allow the protective distancing, and quietly hold the belief in the ongoing movement toward more connection. But it is important not to force connection on the client. Rather, the therapist must follow the client's lead and let the client establish safe distance and be present, knowing this is a part of the journey into greater connection (Herman, 1992). For PTSD clients, learning to discern which relationships are growth fostering and which are not is an important part of their healing. It is also important that they feel they are in charge of regulating the amount of closeness and vulnerability that occurs.

Relational–cultural therapy posits that chronic disconnection is at the core of most human suffering. Combining an understanding of neurobiology with an appreciation of how much we all need healthy connection, RCT practitioners have effectively helped trauma survivors begin to move out of isolation (Banks, 2006a, 2006b). Birrell and Freyd (2006) emphasized the importance of relationship as the context through which trauma can be healed; they proposed an ethic of compassion and mutuality to inform the healing. Gómez, Lewis, Noll, Smidt, and Birrell (2016) also addressed the importance of relational care.

Banks (2006b) developed RCT guidelines for working with trauma. Specifically, she provided insights and practical interventions for reworking the neurological sequelae of trauma (Banks, 2016). She also examined how the physiological destruction of childhood abuse contributes to chronic disconnections (Banks, 2006b). Vicario, Tucker, Smith-Adcock, and Hudgins-Mitchell (2013) developed relational–cultural play therapy, particularly devoted to creating healthy connections with children exposed to trauma in relationships.

Substance Abuse

Covington and Surrey have elaborated on the use of RCT therapy in treating substance abuse in women (Covington, 1994, 1999; Covington & Surrey, 2000; Jordan & Dooley, 2000). Often women begin to use substances in an effort to make or maintain relationships. Ironically, turning to substances to maintain relationships ultimately leads to increased isolation and shame, and addiction itself becomes a kind of encompassing relationship. Women who are at high risk for substance abuse are often socially isolated to begin with; this isolation increases when shame pushes the individual further away from healing connection.

Mutual-help groups such as Alcoholics Anonymous (AA) and Al-Anon reflect the relational model. Mutuality is emphasized, there is absence of hierarchy, and people both receive and provide help (Covington, 1994; Kilbourne, 1999). An outpatient substance abuse treatment program for women that was established using RCT therapy boasted low levels of recidivism (Finkelstein, 1996; Markoff & Cawley, 1996). Counselors working with substance abuse have found RCT's understanding of addiction helpful and compatible with AA precepts (Covington, 1999). Covington (2008) developed a protocol and formal curriculum for treating women with substance abuse that is based in RCT. She also developed a trauma-informed approach noting the high incidence of childhood abuse for women suffering with addictions. She suggested as most useful an integrative treatment model based on RCT, addiction theory, and trauma theory (Covington, 2008). Armstrong (2008) observed that RCT can provide the foundation for a gender-based treatment model for women in recovery from chemical dependency. Noting that the first treatment program specific to women opened in 1975, Armstrong urged that RCT be used as a framework for nursing research on addiction. Koehn (2010) reviewed a relational approach to counseling women with alcohol and other drug problems and noted that RCT is effective in counseling women who misuse alcohol and other drugs. The U.S. State Department has made use of relational–cultural treatment in working with alcoholism in Afghan women (D. Finger Wright, personal communication, June 2012).

Eating Disorders

RCT therapy has been used effectively in the treatment of eating disorders (Tantillo, 1998, 2000, 2006; Tantillo & Sanftner, 2003; see also Chapter 5, this volume). RCT therapy suggests that a woman's disturbances in her relationship with food and in her relationships with herself and others occur largely because of the absence of perceived mutuality. Women with low levels of mutuality are more apt to develop eating disorders (Sanftner et al., 2006). Treatment facilitates an understanding of connections between a woman's relationships with others, with herself, and with food and contributes to developing improved perceived mutuality in relationships with others (Sanftner & Tantillo, 2001; Tantillo, Sanftner, Noyes, & Zippier, 2003). The benefit of thoughtful use of self-disclosure is viewed as one factor in the efficacy of RCT therapy with clients who have eating disorders (Tantillo, 2004). Changes in patients' perceptions of mutuality with their mothers have been seen to increase over the course of a partial hospital stay (Sanftner, Tantillo, & Seidlitz, 2004).

The cultural pressure for thinness is also taken into account in work with young women who suffer from eating disorders (Dooley, 2000; Kilbourne, 1999). Progressive disconnection and isolation, including the secrecy involved with bingeing and purging, contribute to depression and shame. Eating disorders are difficult and complicated problems to overcome in part because of the shame and secrecy surrounding the behaviors. RCT has been particularly useful in understanding and treating eating disorders (Trepal, Boie, & Kress, 2012). In the field of disordered eating research, there is an emphasis on moving from disconnection to mutuality (Sanftner et al., 2006; Tantillo, 2006).

In a study of women with eating disorders, Tantillo and Sanftner (2003) researched the effectiveness of short-term relational group therapy compared with short-term cognitive behavioral group therapy; they also examined the relationship between perceived mutuality of relationships and severity of bulimic and depressive symptoms. They found that relational–cultural short-term therapy, focused primarily on relational factors instead of eating behavior, is effective in treating bulimic symptoms and depression. Work in the area of RCT therapy and eating disorders suggests that eating disorders are diseases of disconnection caused and maintained by disconnections from oneself and others in women with certain biopsychosocial risk factors. Lack of perceived mutuality in relationships is seen as contributing significantly to the etiology and maintenance of women's mental health problems, such as eating disorders (Tantillo et al., 2003). Recovery requires that participants experience increases in perceived mutuality in relationships with important others; this decreases a sense of disconnection.

Sanftner and Tantillo (2004) constructed the Connection–Disconnection Scale (CDS) to assess perceived mutuality in both community and clinical samples of women with eating disorders. The CDS, which is based in RCT, has been found to be a reliable and valid measure of perceived mutuality that can enrich relational understanding. Furthermore, Tantillo and Sanftner (2010a) found significant validation of the use of the measure for both men and women; this self-report measure to assess perceived mutuality experienced in close relationships showed good discrimination and convergent validity.

Tantillo, Sanftner, and Hauenstein (2013) examined the importance of restoring connection in the face of disconnection in treating anorexia nervosa. Additional studies have also looked at family functioning in predicting eating disorder symptoms. Multifamily therapy groups are helpful in moving toward greater mutuality in connection (Sanftner et al., 2006; Tantillo, 2006). Low mutuality with mothers and fathers predicted body dissatisfaction in both men and women, whereas low mutuality with romantic partners predicted body dissatisfaction in women (Sanftner, Ryan, & Pierce, 2009). Sanftner and Tantillo (2001) also conducted an intervention and research project in which they looked at both perceived mutuality and motivation for change in participants in a relational–motivational group for treatment of eating disorders. They found that an emphasis on improving mutuality in relationships with mothers may be an important factor in shifting a patient's motivation for change. Shame in RCT is seen as a major source driving isolation and therefore negatively affects the ability to make use of relationships to heal (Jordan, 1989; Sanftner & Tantillo, 2011; Trepal, Boie, & Kress, 2012). Several researchers have looked at the impact of shame on women with eating disorders: Tantillo and Kreipe (2011) emphasized the importance of improving connections for adolescents across high-intensity settings; Tantillo and Sanftner (2010b) underscored the power of mutuality for patients dealing with eating disorders and their families; and Trepal, Boie, Kress, and Hammer (2015) explored the issues of disconnections and mutuality in treating eating disorders using RCT.

Adolescence

Cannon, Hammer, Reicherzer, and Gilliam (2012) suggested that RCT provides a framework for developing relational competencies and movement in group work with adolescent girls. Lenz, Speciale, and Aguilar (2012) examined RCT interventions with incarcerated adolescents and found that RCT was effective for promoting relational empowerment and engagement with others. Sassen (2012) explored interventions to promote empathic connection and literacy in children. Chhabra (2006) ran "healing conversations" between Hindu and Muslim Pakistani youth where RCT was used to analyze the data and explore the role of youth as peace-builders. Working with Arab and Israeli youths, Morray and Liang

(2005) found that engaging students in RCT-based groups can promote mutual empathy, empowerment, and conflict tolerance between individuals and groups that are disparate. Several programs to empower girls have used different aspects of relational–cultural practice. N. M. Brown (2010) looked at girls in middle school to see how relational development might enhance self-esteem.

A framework for relational competencies in group work with adolescent girls was outlined by Cannon, Hammer, Reicherzer, and Gilliam (2012). Cannon et al. used RCT to address relational aggression, particularly cyberbullying. These authors concluded that the value of RCT is in dismantling lateral marginalization by fostering members' mutual empathy and yearning for change. Downs (2012) examined relational–cultural ways to reduce the stigma among suicidal young adults. McWhirter, Valdez, and Caban (2013) suggested that, in working with Latina adolescents, there be increased access to adult advocates in schools and families and that relational–cultural modes of career intervention be used. Schumacher (2014) created *talking circles* for adolescent girls in an urban high school, a restorative practices program for building friendship and developing emotional literacy skills. These talking circles were grounded in the theoretical frameworks of both RCT and restorative justice. Four relational themes emerged: a joy of being together, feeling safe with each other and free to express genuine emotions, cultivating empathy along with an improved capacity to listen, and showing more sensitivity to herself.

Resilience

Jordan (1992, 2013) has reviewed recent research on resilience and gender, positing that resilience resides not in the individual but in the capacity for connection. Resilience is often portrayed as an internal trait that allows one to "bounce back" from unfortunate situations. RCT has instead conceptualized resilience as a characteristic that arises in relationship (Hartling, 2008; Jordan, 1992, 2013). Hartling (2008) addressed the importance of strengthening resilience in a risky world, concluding that it's all about relationships.

Jordan (1992, 2006) put forward a theory that resilience is a relational phenomenon arising within a relational context. Moving away from individualistic notions of "inner strength," fortitude, and standing strong alone, RCT constructs a model of resilience that depends on our ability to move into relationship to heal and flourish. Resilience is built on supported vulnerability and mutuality (Jordan, 1992, 2006).

Hospice and Grief Work

RCT therapy has been used successfully in hospice work and grief work (Duffey, 2006; Gibson, 2007; Wells, 2005). In grief work, one can validate that grief is a testament to the power and importance of the lost connection. There are profound but nonprescribed feelings when important relationships are lost. That is, we cannot dictate how grief will unfold, only that it will likely disrupt "normal" functioning because the grieving person's very being is affected by the loss of an important relationship. RCT therapy recognizes that we are vulnerable to loss of loved ones. If we are supported in our sadness and grief, we can often find solace and comfort in our remaining relationships. If, however, we are not given room to grieve, or if the culture prescribes unrealistic expectations for grief, often the sadness will go underground. In such cases, depression may set in. Although sadness can provide a path back toward connection, depression often leads to more chronic disconnection. Paying attention to these relational and cultural variables allows clients more room to find their way back into connection.

Working With the Effects of Marginalization

As previously noted, RCT can be especially helpful in elucidating the effects of marginalization, exclusion, and "power over." M. Walker (1999) suggested that in the process of marginalization, the dominant culture distorts images of self, of other, and of relational possibilities. Collins (2000) noted that the dominant culture promotes negative relational and controlling images of the nondominant group by normalizing the process of systematic oppression (see also Thomas & Sillen, 1972). RCT, unlike many theoretical approaches, acknowledges the profound importance of culture, race, racism, social class, and sexual orientation. Thus, the power of the larger context is factored into every understanding of individual disconnection (Jordan, Walker, & Hartling, 2004; Ossana, Helms, & Leonard, 1992; Patton & Reicherzer, 2010; Penzerro, 2007). Because RCT attends carefully to power dynamics and emphasizes the importance of context, it is especially suited to working with diverse and differing cultural, racial, ethnic, and sexual orientation groups. Often the therapist notes that societal factors most potently disempower the client in a particular situation. The power of social exclusion and shaming is often overlooked when the individual or her or his mother or family is seen as the total source of the problem. Socioeconomic context dramatically influences personal development.

Counseling Psychology

RCT has been embraced by many counseling psychologists (Comstock, 2005). Comstock (2005; Comstock et al., 2008) in particular has worked on bridging relational, multicultural, and social justice competencies. She noted that RCT provides a framework for looking at sex-role socialization, power, dominance, marginalization, and subordination as they affect the mental health and relational development of all people. RCT offers ways for counselors to think about the development of empathy: "Promising guidance for facilitating the development of the capacious, unflinching empathy that will be needed in this century is offered in Relational-Cultural theory of psychotherapy and relational development" (Montgomery & Kottler, 2005, p. 98). Duffey and Somody (2011) suggested that RCT provides a useful model for counseling, given the multicultural paradigm that the counseling field embraces. Headley and Sangganjanavanich (2014) provided basic guidelines for using key concepts and structures to create interventions based on RCT. In their *Handbook of Counseling Women*, Kopala and Keitel (2003) noted that "the vast majority of clients who seek counseling are women, and although numerous books address the psychology of women, no handbooks are solely devoted to counseling women on the array of issues that we confront in modern day society" (p. xi). RCT is cited as an approach that addresses that lack (Jordan, 2003; Kopala & Keitel, 2017).

One issue with the use of RCT in counseling psychology is that the wider challenge of this model to existing paradigms of separate-self psychology has often been overlooked (Ivey, D'Andrea, Ivey, & Simek-Morgan, 2007). However, Pedersen, Crethar, and Carlson's (2008) work on *inclusive cultural empathy* contributed substantially to establishing the importance of the social context and the importance of power arrangements. Like RCT, these authors' work placed culture at the center of understanding individual development.

Supervision and Training

RCT has been used in many training programs in psychology, counseling, social work, and nursing. RCT supervision invites the supervisor to practice relational sensitivity and respect and to use the core RCT concepts to understand therapy dynamics. Downs (2006) noted that "emphasizing the centrality of connection brings into focus the complexity and texture of the many, intersecting relationships that are part of psychotherapy and supervisory practice" (p. 3). In RCT, the supervisor attends to the relationship between supervisee and client but also acknowledges the larger framework of relationships that influence the supervision process (e.g., professional contacts). As Downs (2006) pointed out, the supervisor is one "whose power is used to create a space for a mutual, reflective process" (p. 8). The learning process in supervision involves mutual influence (Montgomery & Kottler, 2005). Both people need to be open enough to the impact of the other so that real change can come about within the supervision relationship itself. It is important that the supervisee feel safe enough to share the vulnerabilities and uncertainties that can arise in the treatment setting. It is often useful for supervisors to share examples of difficult therapy situations from their own professional development and, in so doing, model active problem-solving as well as dispel fantasies of supervisor omnipotence. As

Downs (2006) noted, we need to pay attention to the "space between— between thoughts and action, certainty and doubt, teaching and learning, and question and answer" (p. 11). Rock (1997) conducted a series of survey studies that showed students experience good supervisors as those who are attuned to both their learning and emotional needs.

Relational–cultural supervision focuses on essential RCT practices (language, conceptualization, and therapeutic techniques) and processes (moving toward connection and authenticity, fostering mutual empathy, and supporting vulnerability). RCT focuses on building relational resilience and acknowledging social context (Lenz, 2014). Additionally, Pack (2009) suggested that RCT provides a useful model for supervision.

RECENT NONCLINICAL APPLICATIONS

Although the RCT model was developed to explain the psychology of women and to alter clinical practices that were seen as potentially disempowering or hurtful to women, its reach has extended far beyond its origins. RCT quickly pointed to the need for a better understanding of all people. It also sought to delineate the effects of stratification and marginalization on the individual and on social groups (with a clear social justice agenda). Today there are several promising areas of theoretical expansion for RCT. Some of these are already yielding useful intervention strategies.

For example, RCT offers insight into the importance of friends in women's lives. Relationships are core to our sense of well-being and contribute to our growth in multiple ways. The Girls Circle Program addresses the importance of building social support for adolescent girls (Hossfeld, 2008). Cannon et al. (2012) suggested that RCT is useful in addressing relational aggression, cyberbullying, and fostering mutual empathy. Comas-Diaz and Weiner (2013) examined how women's friendships heal them. Frey, Beesley, Hurst, Saldana, and Licuanan (2016) studied the growth-supporting relational qualities in same-sex friendships of college women and men.

Another area of growing RCT research is with incarcerated individuals. Emerson and Ramaswamy (2015) turned to RCT to inform trauma-specific interventions for incarcerated women. Looking through the lens of RCT, social capital, and feminist inquiry, Pickering (2014) addressed the importance of challenging community ideas about women released from prison. Bell (2008) studied the relational patterns between African American mothers in correctional supervision and maternal caregiving grandmothers. Cannon et al. (Cannon, 2007; Cannon et al., 2012) used relational practice groups with a population of relationally aggressive adolescent females.

Organizational Applications

Another important and vast area for future expansion is in the application of RCT to organizations, in particular, through new models of leadership, creativity in the workplace, and recognition of the importance of relational skills in effective workplaces (Brimm, 2010; Jordan, 1999). Goleman (1997) pointed to the significant role of emotional intelligence in the workplace, and Senghe (1990) addressed the importance of a two-way flow of information in what he called the *learning organization*. Neither of these approaches has explicitly addressed power, gender, and diversity, which would be a fruitful area for future exploration. Fletcher (1999) noted the ways in which extremely important relational skills are made invisible in organizations and suggests that the practice of fluid expertise, empathic teaching, and mutuality can contribute to a greater effectiveness in the workplace. Using RCT as a base theory (Fletcher, 1999, 2004; Fletcher, Jordan, & Miller, 2000), Fletcher has outlined several crucial skills for transforming the workplace into a more relational environment: empathic competence, emotional competence, authenticity, fluid expertise, vulnerability, embedding outcome, holistic thinking, and response-ability. Fletcher (2004) named four types of relational practice: (a) preserving, or relational activities that are meant to preserve the life and well-being of a project; (b) mutual empowering, or assisting others' achievement and contributions to the project; (c) achieving, or using relational skills to increase one's own effectiveness; and (d) creating team through activities intended to create an atmosphere of collegiality, where the positive outcomes of group life can occur (p. 272).

Attention to the forces of marginalization and how a work culture deals with "difference" among its workers will become increasingly important as the workforce becomes more diverse. Building on existing RCT work on organizations has the potential to offer useful theoretical and practical insights into these issues. Motulsky (2010) used RCT to elucidate processes in career transitions. Fletcher (2012) pursued, with others, the development of a relational model of leadership. Through an RCT lens, she explored positive relationships at work and developed a model of leadership as a particular kind of positive relationship at work. Hartling and Sparks (2008) addressed the dilemmas of staying connected in a disconnecting work context. Jordan and Romney (2005) applied RCT to consulting around diversity, authenticity, and mutual empowerment in corporate settings. Portman and Garrett (2005) explored the leadership approaches in American Indian cultures, noting some resonance with RCT.

Understanding Boys and Men

Although early RCT development dealt primarily with representing women's psychological experience more accurately, RCT has also looked at men's experience. Bergman (1991, 1996) has noted that for men there may be a kind of "relational dread," a sense of incompetence in the relational realm. Pollack (1998) noted that boys have strong yearnings for connection, similar to their female counterparts, but that rigid sex-role expectations, often experienced as traumatic, limit the full expression of these yearnings. There are indications that boys in the dominant culture are disconnected early from many of their feelings, particularly those suggesting vulnerability. As Pollack described, gender-role socialization for boys often involves a severe code of behavior that amounts to a traumatic disconnection. Shame exerts a powerful force on boys and men (Levant & Pollack, 1995; Pleck, 1981; Pollack, 1998), and powerful pressures for disconnection influence boys' development.

This work points to new ways of intervening with boys and men in therapy (Hoffman, 1977; Kiselica, Englar-Carlson, & Horne, 2008) and has been helpful to parents of sons who value sensitivity and connectedness in their children. Dooley and Fedele (1999) paid particular attention to the mother–son relationship and the challenges involved in raising boys who can stay connected with the full range of their feelings and with other people beyond the scripts that society imposes on them. Dooley has run relational groups for 10-year-old boys. Dooley and Fedele have conducted workshops for mothers and sons of all ages. In this work, mothers often express enormous pain around their efforts to support their sons' sensitivity and empathy as they also try to prepare them for social worlds that largely mock or scorn male vulnerability. Lombardi (2011) wrote about the abiding closeness between mothers and sons that offers a boy a sense of strength and allows sensitivity; she examines the destructive consequences of our cultural push for boys to "stand alone" and deny any feelings of dependency or vulnerability. In particular, boys and mothers are shamed if their attachment to each other is seen as undermining the boy's "masculinity."

Additional research has recently been conducted on the use of RCT with boys and men by Englar-Carlson, Evans, and Duffey (2014), who studied female counselors using RCT with men and also examined the nature of the connections, disconnections, and reconnections that frame men's lives (Englar-Carlson, Stevens, & Scholz, 2010). Duffey and Haberstroh (2014) addressed the use of developmental relational counseling with men. In *A Counselor's Guide to Working With Men* (Englar-Carlson et al., 2014), RCT is presented as contextually focused and culture driven. The reader is introduced to the role of authenticity in work with men and the value of bidirectional empathy. Englar-Carlson et al. (2010) and Frey and Melrath-Dyer (2005) have also presented research on a useful relational perspective for working with aggressive youth and youth with sexual behavioral problems.

Relational Parenting

RCT has clear relevance for parenting. Most of the traditional theories of child development and parenting promote a heavy bias toward independence training. Thus, babies are expected to sleep alone, spend a lot of time physically separated from parents, and exercise increasing independent control of their needs. Most contemporary popular parenting manuals embody the values of independence and autonomy. Martha and William Sears (Sears & Sears, 2001) have suggested we consider "attachment parenting" instead. Focusing on the importance of attachment, they have emphasized responsiveness and maintaining physical closeness and have pointed out that other cultures encourage far more ongoing physical and emotional connection between mother and child.

A model of relational parenting (Jordan, 1998; see also Chapter 5, this volume) has been suggested. It emphasizes encouraging empathy, differentiating mutual from nonmutual relationships, appreciating the capacity for good conflict, and growing around difference. Relational parenting promotes the development of clarity by helping children develop personal awareness and differentiating thoughts, feelings, and actions. It also promotes awareness of others, teaching that awareness and sensitivity to others' feelings, needs, and communications are an essential part of psychological growth. There is an emphasis on helping children develop listening and communication skills. Awareness of relationship dynamics is a part of this general relationship learning. Children are reminded to care about relationships and the impact of their actions on others. Parents also assist children in assessing which relationships are "safe," where they can be vulnerable and take small and appropriate relational risks. Children also need help discerning where caution in relationship is necessary. Mutual empathy and engagement and a desire to serve the community are values that are actively encouraged, and the myth of the superiority of competition and autonomous achievement is questioned.

Respect for difference and honoring diversity is central to socializing any child. Children are taught to think critically about the messages the culture provides, including overuse of violence to solve problems, an emphasis on consumerism, and the use of damaging labels and attitudes toward people who are not in the dominant mainstream. This includes paying attention to the distortions created by sexism, racism, and other prejudicial practices. There is a premium on taking responsibility in relationships and on honoring each person's dignity. Children can learn to differentiate growth-fostering and non–growth-fostering relationships, and parents can help children develop this skill. Where possible, relational resilience is supported; this involves helping a child negotiate hurt feelings or acute disconnections in a way that eventually facilitates reconnection.

Relational parenting seeks to undermine the extreme gender stereotypes that exist for most children (Watson-Phillips, 2007). It also attempts to reduce the experience of shame wherever possible. Children are taught to differentiate safe from unsafe contexts, an approach used by parents of marginalized groups who have to actively teach their children to be bicultural. Thus, Greene (1990) documented the ways that African American mothers teach their children to survive in a racist culture by helping them learn where they can show which aspects of themselves and where they need to establish safety by disconnecting or being less transparent. For survival reasons, marginalized and oppressed groups and mothers have to teach their children strategic management of vulnerability and contextual vigilance.

Many parents are naturally uncomfortable with mainstream parenting manuals and advice that push children toward premature independence, competitiveness, and stereotyped gender roles. It is hoped that this model of relational parenting, together with the movement toward attachment parenting, will continue to provide alternative methods of raising children; in particular, we want to give children the message that we all need love and connection throughout our lives, that none of us can thrive alone, and that loving relationships can serve as places of growth and well-being for all of us. Relational values and practices have the potential to transform not just families, but our entire hyperindividualistic society.

Relational–Cultural Ethics

Practicing from an RCT perspective requires a rethinking of ethics and ethical principles. Birrell (2006) posed the following questions: What does it mean to be ethical in psychotherapy? Does adherence to ethical codes and rules make a psychotherapist ethical? Birrell suggested that ethics should not be an afterthought but the primary consideration of clinical utility. She added that in avoiding "what it means to be truly ethical, we run the risk of conflating ethics with risk management, mistaking rules for relationships, and damaging those very people whom we so desperately want to help" (Birrell, 2006, p. 95).

Birrell and Bruns (2016) examined the existing code of ethics put forth by the American Counseling Association and proposed instead a relational ethic, grounded in RCT. It is by engaging in relationship, rather than rules, that counselors exercise ethical practice.

WHAT'S AHEAD?

Neurobiology of Relationship

Perhaps the most exciting work that validates RCT concepts is current research on neuroscience and relationship. Although this body of work has been developed independently of RCT, it supports almost every principle and precept that RCT began developing 30 years ago. With new technology for registering brain functioning, we will be able to track the movement of mutual responsiveness and empathy between therapist and client, parent and child, and friend and friend. We will be able to assess which interactions enhance growth and which may interfere with personal change. Although we are close to being able to do this with functional magnetic resonance imaging (fMRI) and positron emission tomography (PET) scans, the technology is still intrusive and bulky. In this ongoing research, it is likely we will continue to find substantial validation of the core concepts of RCT.

In fact, the field of neuroscience has already provided broad and robust validation for RCT. In *Wired to Connect*, Amy Banks (2016) presented a straightforward, compelling, and easy-to-understand explication of the way in which we are neurologically primed to flourish in connection with others. Banks also has developed a C.A.R.E. scale (calm, acceptedness, resonance, energy) to help people chart relational resources and determine in which relationships they can safely risk more vulnerability and openness and hence experience more growth and emotional well-being. Her work is built on RCT and on the burgeoning discoveries through fMRI studies of the great plasticity of the brain and the ways in which relationships with others shape our brain structure and function (Banks, 2016; Cozolino, 2014;

Doidge, 2007; Eisenberger & Lieberman, 2005; Eisenberger, Lieberman, & Williams, 2003; Porges, 2011; Siegel, 2010).

Need for Research on Clinical Outcomes

A pressing concern for RCT and RCT therapy is further research into its clinical efficacy. Although there is an active research network spawning projects that use RCT, there is a relative absence of a solid body of clinical outcome research using the model. Such research would greatly contribute to the expanding application of the model. Recently Lenz (2016) summarized the outcome studies on RCT therapy. He found clear support for positive change. However, additional outcome research is needed to underscore the usefulness of RCT in treating differently challenged and suffering individuals.

RCT remains dedicated to analysis of power dynamics and social justice and will continue to contribute to the development of more effective therapy. As change agents, RCT practitioners pursue ever more clarity regarding what leads to change in therapy, families, everyday relationships, and cultures. There is an intensifying urgency for the development of growth-fostering relationships, an appreciation of the common good, and the importance of meaning systems developed in community. Many people are struggling to find hope—to find ways to honor their own and others' needs to engage in mutual relationships. We need to contribute to the well-being of others, to fulfill our human nature to be connected, empathic, and part of something larger. Additional research similar to the Toronto study by Oakley et al. (2013) will be important to show the effectiveness of RCT on clinical outcomes.

Social Justice and Power

More recently, in line with the original social justice interests of Jean Baker Miller, RCT theorists have been using RCT to broaden our understanding of race, oppression, marginalization, and many other areas. Cholewa et al. (2014) conducted an examination of culturally responsive educational practices on the psychological well-being of students of color. Edwards,

Bryant, and Clark (2008) studied the ways in which African American female social work educators can thrive in a predominantly White school of social work. Hoffnung (2005) addressed therapy in the interest of social justice, seeing RCT as engaged in a larger critique of social arrangements that benefit dominant groups and pathologize marginalized groups. Jordan wrote several articles addressing issues involved in social change: *Learning at the Margin* (Jordan, 2008b), *Valuing Vulnerability: New Definitions of Courage* (Jordan, 2008e), and *Commitment to Connection in a Culture of Fear* (Jordan, 2008a). M. Walker (2008a, 2008b) suggested we adopt Miller's notion of power as the capacity to produce change. She noted that culture is stratified along multiple dimensions (race, class, sexual orientation, to name a few). When differences are stratified and power-over dynamics prevail, the exercise of power often contributes to maintaining the status quo. These dynamics also contribute to isolation and immobilization among those at the margin. The emphasis on power and social justice distinguishes RCT from most other contemporary clinical theories. RCT acknowledges the importance of the social context in creating growth and well-being or dysfunction and pain. RCT also advocates that as change agents, therapists have a responsibility to address the societal forces that create such significant pain for so many people.

Education

Increasingly, RCT principles are being introduced in educational systems. Tucker, Smith-Adcock, and Trepal (2011) guide middle school counselors in applying RCT in their work. Research by T. J. Carter (2012) suggested relational practice in the adult learning classroom could be based on RCT principles. Hossfeld (2008) noted the success of the Girls Circle Program, a gender-specific, relational–cultural empowerment model for girls' healthy development within a peer support group. Gu and Day (2007) viewed teachers' career-long commitment and effectiveness as related to their relational resilience. Schwartz and Holloway (2012, 2014) studied the importance to educational success of mutuality between teachers and adult students.

Marginalization

New applications of RCT to doctoral advising and to higher education are being put forth, especially with students from underrepresented (marginalized) backgrounds. Close, supportive relationships with a faculty member have been found to be important; students lacking supportive relationships with faculty experience feelings of isolation and marginalization (Protivnak & Foss, 2009). RCT is a fitting conceptual framework for advising relationships aimed at increasing the relational support for underrepresented doctoral students, specifically because it is responsive to and inclusive of multicultural considerations (Comstock et al., 2008; Jordan, 2010; Ruiz, 2012). The RCT framework can be used as an important pedagogical tool to help the advisor understand the challenges encountered by the advisee as a result of her or his racial/ethnic/cultural background and explore experience of discrimination, marginalization, and oppression. RCT differs from other clinical and developmental theories, precisely because of the emphasis placed on the larger cultural and social context (Frey, 2013; Purgason, Avent, Cashwell, Jordan, & Reese, 2016; West, 2005).

Purgason et al. (2016) noted that *anticipatory empathy*—anticipating what the other person is experiencing based on knowledge of that individual and the individual's contextual experiences—is important in building growth-fostering relationships. Authenticity is difficult in relationships where one member holds a culturally privileged identity and the other a culturally oppressed identity. Those with privilege and "power over" often suppress the voices of those who hold a different view of reality or seek a different distribution of power. The experience and worldview of the oppressed or marginalized are often treated as inferior to those of the privileged.

Although RCT continues to be useful in the practice of psychotherapy, it is increasingly being viewed as providing a lens through which we can arrive at a more accurate and positive understanding of human nature. As such, it opens the way for applying the values and precepts of RCT to developmental theory, educational practice, principles of social justice, sociopolitical policy, economic scholarship, mentoring, studies of health, and empowerment. The principle of growing and healing through mutual empathy stimulates hope, a sense of encouragement, the capacity to contribute to the larger community, and an appreciation of the importance of attending to the common good. The more we acknowledge the centrality of connection to our individual and collective well-being, the more we will begin to get free of the dilemma of coming into the world hardwired for connection but having to live in a culture that lauds individual, competitive achievement and trivializes the power of connection in our lives. In the existing system, strength is synonymous with autonomy and an ethic of "stand on your own"; the need for others is seen as the epitome of weakness. The culture calls for independence; our neurobiology seeks interdependence. New models of strength and well-being embrace our ultimate interdependence, our desire to be in mutual connection, a state in which the growth of both people in a relationship matters. Ultimately, RCT values the growth of caring communities and contexts of mutuality that support our creativity, sense of meaning, and ultimate well-being in connection.

7

Summary

Relational–cultural theory (RCT) has grown over the past four decades from a model intended to better represent the psychology of women into a theory that proposes a new relational paradigm of psychology applicable to all people. RCT points out that traditional Western psychologies have overemphasized the study of the separate self and underemphasized the centrality of relationship and the power of context in people's development. These traditional models have also minimized the power of socioeconomic, racial, gender, and other marginalizing variables to distort, debilitate, and disconnect people. These disconnections at the personal and societal levels have created untold suffering, including economic drain and profound disempowerment.

The separation bias in psychology arose at its inception. To demonstrate its scientific validity, psychology as a young discipline emulated the then-reigning field of Newtonian physics, which studied what were seen as

http://dx.doi.org/10.1037/0000063-007
Relational–Cultural Therapy, Second Edition, by J. V. Jordan
Copyright © 2018 by the American Psychological Association. All rights reserved.

essentially discrete entities (molecules and atoms) that secondarily came together to form new entities. Ironically as psychology sought to shore up its respectability by identifying with Newtonian physics, the "new" quantum physics was already pointing to relationships rather than atoms as the natural unit of study and the ultimate reality.

RCT and other theoretical groups are in the process of accomplishing a similarly essential paradigm shift from separation psychology to relational psychology (Belenky, Clinchy, Goldberger, & Tarule, 1986; L. M. Brown, 1998; Gilligan, 1982; Jack, 1991; Mitchell, 1988; Pipher, 1994; Trepal & Duffey, 2016). What distinguishes and differentiates RCT is its persistent emphasis on the importance of context, most specifically the ways in which power dynamics affect human interactions. The study of relationships extends way beyond the dyadic, nuclear family or even the extended family. RCT views the individual as existing within a social context, which either contributes to a sense of connection and empowerment or shapes an experience of disempowerment and disconnection. Thus, forces of stratification and invalidation are seen not only as personally hurtful and damaging but as eroding possible communal sources of support and growth. RCT bridges the relational, cultural, and social realms, and increasingly it is bolstering its theoretical underpinnings by integrating validating psychobiological data.

In the realm of psychotherapy, the relational psychoanalysts (Aron, 1996; Mitchell, 1988) have made an active effort to move from a *one-person psychology* to a *two-person psychology*. Some use language quite similar to RCT regarding mutuality. Robert Stolorow's (Stolorow & Atwood, 1992) theoretical exploration of intersubjectivity has much in common with RCT, but the actual practice of relational psychoanalysis seems to rely less on the real relationship and more on the development of insight to bring about change. This differs from the RCT therapy emphasis on the actual alteration of the experience of isolation in the therapeutic relationship. These theories also do not appear to actively grapple with the question of a separate self, nor do they provide an analysis of power and societal forces of stratification.

Most psychodynamic therapies have similarly moved from a traditional one-person psychology to a two-person psychology in understanding the process of therapy (Safran & Muran, 2000). Yet many of these therapies still adhere to the notion that change is created by resolving unconscious conflict and making the unconscious conscious largely through analytic or interpretative means. To the extent that the relationship is implicated in healing, it is often given a supporting but not central role. For instance, it is referred to as the *therapeutic alliance*, which must be in place for the "deep" work of resolving unconscious conflict to take place. In other words, creating the therapeutic alliance and using one's empathy to understand and thus elucidate conflicts is viewed as important for building a more solid, bounded self. The technical work of behavior modification also recognizes the need for a good-enough relationship between therapist and client to move forward. Cognitive behavior therapy is also useful in bringing about changes that may allow a client to begin to effectively seek connection and manage affect or impulses that might interfere with that movement.

RCT therapy, in contrast, points to the centrality of healing in the therapeutic relationship itself. Empathy is used not just to understand the person (although that is important) but also to lessen the sense of isolation. Mutual empathy creates change. We feel seen, known, and understood when we experience empathy from others. And importantly, we feel less alone. We feel joined. We feel kinship. We feel less shame, more self-worth. We feel more alive and hopeful, more able to think, to move, to change. Our authentic feelings and voices begin to find expression. Finding voice is a dialogic experience. Our voice does not emerge from within a separate, inner self. Rather, it is cocreated by speaker and listener. As I am listened to empathically and responsively, I can bring more and more of my authentic experience into voice, into relationship. Voice is a metaphor, as is the self. But unlike self, which often gets concretized and seen as organized in separation, voice is a relational metaphor. Empathic listening also supports the emergence of an expanded representation of one's experience, literally giving voice to more and more of one's feelings and thoughts. Both the listening and the speaking are active, empowering processes. We are literally "listened into voice." We listen others into voice, into action, into hope. We have a need to participate in growth-fostering relationships; our need is for mutuality.

The neurobiological data strongly support the notion that we need connections to grow and thrive. In fact, new data indicate that we need connection to survive throughout our lives; we never outgrow our need for connection (Banks, 2016; Lieberman, 2013). We come into the world primed to seek mutual connection; our brains grow, and there is balance between sympathetic and parasympathetic functioning when there is sufficient early mutuality between infant and caregiver and an absence of chronic stress. However, our social conditioning with its overvaluing of separation, autonomy, and independence is at odds with our underlying biological predispositions. Herein lies a profound dilemma, as these competing tendencies produce enormous stress in all of us. Our individualistic social conditioning erodes the very community that our biology suggests we need. We are neurologically wired to connect (to thrive in relationship) but taught to stand strong alone (to be independent and autonomous). Stress is created at a chronic and undermining level when standards for maturity that cannot actually be attained with any predictability are placed on people. Thus, we are told to be strong through autonomy and separation. But in fact, "going it alone," or being on the outside, creates pain and a sense of inadequacy. We are told not to be vulnerable, particularly if we are male; and yet every day we encounter the inevitability of our vulnerability. We see loved ones get sick or die; we watch our children suffer with illnesses that we cannot always cure. We watch parents and loved ones succumb to the indignities of older age. We hear of random acts of violence felling adolescent boys in the inner city, of children starving in Africa, of people tortured in prisons. Yet, in our effort to deny our vulnerability, we tend to locate vulnerability in chosen target groups who are then seen as "lesser than." We marginalize and denigrate those who are seen as "weak." We minimize the real pain of exclusion and marginalization.

RCT therapy offers a responsive relationship based on respect and dedication to facilitating movement out of isolation. In this context, people heal from chronic disconnections and begin to rework maladaptive, negative relational images, which are keeping them locked in shame and isolation. Energy is generated, feelings of worth increase, creative activity resumes, and people demonstrate enhanced clarity about their experience and about relationships. Most important, they engage in relationships that contribute to the growth of others and community is supported.

Although we are gaining clarity about what facilitates change in therapy (and change in general), there is an ongoing need for clinicians to persistently revisit the question "What creates positive change in therapy?" It should be a question we ponder with great regularity. We also need to expand our inquiry to "What creates positive change in the world? What can we transfer from the micro level of working with individuals in the rarified atmosphere of psychotherapy to the macro level of groups, societies, the world?" At the same time, we must honor the many questions that we cannot answer about how psychotherapy operates or how we can make a difference in the world (Jordan, 2014). There are many theories, many opinions, many success stories, and many failed therapies. RCT holds that therapists, as self-defined change agents, have a responsibility to pursue questions about social change as well as personal change. Context is essential to an understanding of suffering and what is called pathology, and thus the need for change in the social milieus within which we function must be addressed. Therapists have a special responsibility to question the part that the larger culture plays in creating the disconnections and other suffering that bring people to treatment. They also have a responsibility to facilitate the well-being of the greatest number of people possible.

A criticism of RCT is that its emphasis on the importance of relationships forces individuals to remain in all sorts of relationships, including hurtful, imbalanced, nonmutual, possibly abusive ones (Westkott, 1997). Nothing could be farther from the truth. RCT rests on the premise that we function best in growth-fostering relationships and that we have to work on disconnections and misunderstandings in our relationships. But it does not posit that all relationships are growth-fostering or healthy. In fact, it seeks to help people differentiate what is growth-fostering from what is destructive. It also encourages people to protect themselves and, if necessary, to leave relationships that are injurious or toxic. But it does not tell people to "stand on their own two feet," get over the "pathological dependence," or stop "enabling" others. Instead, the ongoing need for connection is acknowledged and honored, and individuals are supported in finding new relationships to which they can turn and on which they can depend.

We are currently seeing the consequences of a culture of disconnection both physically, in medical ailments and premature death in many men, and emotionally, in extremely high levels of fear, anxiety, depression, and other indicators of chronic stress. One quarter of the people in the United States will suffer from an episode of depression at some point in their lives; another quarter will suffer with clinical anxiety. We also see the impact on societies; there is a dangerous breakdown of community signaled by upswings in isolation and violence and downward trends in community involvement (Putnam, 2000). RCT suggests the way out of this is to really grasp that participating in growth-fostering relationships benefits all participants. It is not a question of self versus other, selfishness versus selflessness. Connection itself needs to be supported and empowered. Communities need to be attended to and nourished. People need to invest in the well-being of others beyond their nuclear families. The dominant culture undermines this awareness, and psychology has unfortunately contributed to the separate-self mentality among those at the "center." Those at the margin are adversely affected by these biases, and their own attempts to commit to community-building are often attacked or mocked ("they" cannot stand on their own).

Helplessness often occurs when people cease to feel that they can make a difference and have an effect on their worlds, human and inanimate. When people feel they don't matter, they lose hope. Immobilization, isolation, self-blame, feeling overwhelmed, and finding no responsiveness in one's context characterize hopelessness. What Seligman (1991) called *learned helplessness* may be the behavioral accompaniment of hopelessness; in human relationships, shame and immobilization ensue from disconnection and lead to further disconnection. Many therapists see a major part of their work as helping clients reestablish a sense of hope. Scientists, philosophers, and theologians have come up with many definitions of hope. Most address the development of positive expectations for the future.

In RCT, hope might best be depicted as the possibility for movement toward an experience of connectedness, growth, and "mattering" to one another. This relational hope may also involve an awareness and belief in the basic connectedness of us all; it tells us that we can have an impact on others and that we can expect others to respond to us in a way that helps us grow and conveys that we matter and make a difference in the relationships we value. Hope arises in relationship. Hope arises where change is deemed possible. Hope arises where one anticipates responsiveness and where dignity and respect prevail. Ironically, at the edge of connection and disconnection, where the challenge to relational hope can be the most daunting, we can also find the possibility for profound growth.

Martin Luther King, Jr. (1967) said, "True compassion is more than flinging a coin to a beggar; it comes to see that an edifice which produces beggars needs restructuring." And George Albee stated, "Only with radical social changes leading to a just society will there be a reduction in the incidence of emotional problems" (Caplan & Cosgrove, 2004, p. ii). With its emphasis on individual psychology and individual pathology, psychology typically feeds into an overly personalized misattribution. RCT calls us to look beyond the individual to understand the relational patterns that arise in the individual's life and the nature of chronic disconnections and disempowerment in the larger culture. RCT invites us to bring whatever small or great wisdom we have about change to the realm of social change. RCT is a profoundly hopeful theory. While it recognizes the power of relationships to violate and hurt, its most important impact is that it recognizes the power of relationships to heal us, to help us grow, to nourish us, to free and empower us. And it recognizes that relationships occur between individuals who are blessed with enormous neuroplasticity and have the capacity to grow and change.

Current technological and neurological advances have the potential to transform not just therapy but society. Positron emission tomography scans and functional magnetic resonance imaging (fMRI) provide access to brain function in ways that are truly amazing. In the coming years, we will undoubtedly have a technology that enables us to routinely record neurological activity occurring simultaneously in both therapist and client (akin to fMRI but without the structural challenges of current brain technologies). We will likely see corresponding brain activation and growth as empathic attunement flows between the two people. We will be able to better locate and name what is happening in the interaction that creates this brain activity, which in turn will improve our ability to teach how most effectively to alter neuronal pathways and subjective emotional experience. We may even discover how to help people directly regulate destructive amygdala responding and develop enhanced empathic abilities. It could be that the aggressive, reactive, trigger-happy responding that often leads to interpersonal injury will be able to be modified by some simple intervention, perhaps learned through fMRI training. Instead of hurtful, retaliatory responses, people may learn how to work on disconnection with a view to the greater good, creating relational resilience and peaceful conflict resolution. Perhaps we will create a social system that values and supports healthy connections and devotes significant energy to achieving social justice.

We are only beginning to explore the vast world of relational responsiveness and the corresponding domains of brains primed to connect and heal. What was put forth as a theory based on listening to women's voices is fast being validated by the field of neuroscience, one of the most respected and sophisticated fields in psychiatry and psychology (Goleman, 2006; Siegel, 1999). The larger culture still holds out impossible images of the advantage of standing alone, against and over others, but more and more, we are learning that we are being pitted against our own true nature of interdependence and of finding safety by building good connection. It is time for this dilemma to be exposed and reworked. A relational psychology that emphasizes our basic need and yearning for connection throughout the lifespan provides such a breakthrough. RCT provides both hope and realistic standards for human development. It supports a revolutionary shift in the dominant culture itself, away from an ethic of competitive self-interest to an ethic of mutual interest that occurs in mutually empathic, growth-fostering relationships. In the end, it is relationships that stimulate neuroplasticity and cognitive/emotional change. And it is connections that support life and creative growth. They lie at the heart of human meaning-making and development.

Glossary of Key Terms

ACUTE DISCONNECTION   A frequent occurrence in relationships resulting from a failure to understand or a sense that the other is not there in a responsive way and sometimes in more actively harmful ways such as humiliation or violation; in therapy, reworking acute disconnections becomes one of the most useful places of change.

AGGRESSION   The use of force to achieve a goal; emotionally, often involves the use of control, "power over" others, or an attempt to hurt or destroy others.

AMYGDALA HIJACK   A term coined by Goleman (1997) to refer to the reactive tracking of a response through the amygdala rather than through the cortex; often involved in heightened reactivity and impulsivity around anger and fear; more common in people with a history of trauma.

ANGER   An important relational feeling that signals "something is wrong"; a necessary part of the movement of relationship, it points to the need for change, whether at a personal or collective level; distinguished from aggression or dominance.

ANTICIPATORY EMPATHY   Using one's attunement to and understanding of an individual to predict the possible impact of one's words
or actions on another person; a therapist constantly tries to use anticipatory empathy to get a sense of what might ensue following a particular intervention in therapy.

AUTHENTICITY   The capacity to bring one's real experience, feelings,
and thoughts into relationship, with sensitivity to and awareness
of the possible impact on others of one's actions. It does not give
license to total reactivity (what we might call *amygdala authenticity*).
Authenticity does not involve telling the "whole truth" but rather sharing the "one true thing" that will move the therapy in some positive
way. Relational authenticity arises in the context of a relationship and
is guided by the intention to participate in a growth-fostering relationship. Anticipatory empathy guides the authentic responsiveness
of the therapist or helping person. In the course of getting to know the
client and paying careful attention, the therapist develops empathic
attunement that leads to an anticipation of the possible impact of his
or her interventions on the client. This allows the client to experience growth-fostering connection, a sense of "mattering"; he or she
experiences firsthand a responsive, intentional growth-fostering relationship. Anticipatory empathy also occurs in relationships outside
therapy and leads to an overall pattern of responsiveness rather than
reactivity and confirms the sense that one is being listened to and
understood.

CENTRAL RELATIONAL PARADOX   In the face of repeated disconnections, people yearn even more for relationship, but their fear of
engaging with others leads to keeping aspects of their experience out
of connection (these are protective strategies of disconnection, also
known as *strategies of survival*). Individuals alter themselves to fit in
with the expectations and wishes of the other person, and in the process, the relationship itself loses authenticity and mutuality, becoming
another source of disconnection.

CHRONIC DISCONNECTION   An escalating and ongoing dynamic in
which the less powerful person in a relationship is prevented from

representing the hurt or disconnection to the more powerful person and learns that she or he cannot bring this aspect of her or his experience into relationship. The less powerful person begins to twist herself to fit into the relationship by becoming more inauthentic and by splitting herself off from these feelings and thoughts. A spiral of disconnection often occurs, and the relationship becomes less mutual, less a place of growth and possibility.

CONDEMNED ISOLATION   A phrase coined by Jean Baker Miller to capture the experience of isolation and aloneness that leaves one feeling shut out of the human community. One feels alone, immobilized regarding reconnection, and at fault for this state. This is different from the experience of "being alone" or solitude, in which one can feel deeply connected (to nature, other people, etc.).

CONNECTION   Although this term is used in common parlance to mean any kind of relationship, RCT defines connection as an interaction between two or more people that is mutually empathic and mutually empowering. It involves emotional accessibility and leads to the "five good things" (zest, worth, productivity, clarity, and desire for more connection).

CONTROLLING IMAGES   Images constructed by the dominant group that represent distortions of the nondominant cultural group being depicted, with the intent of disempowering them. The phrase was coined by Patricia Hill Collins (1990), who noted, "People become objectified to certain categories such as race, gender, economic class and sexual orientation" (p. 228).

DISCONNECTIONS   Interactions in relationships where mutual empathy and mutual empowerment do not occur; usually involves disappointment, a sense of being misunderstood, and sometimes a sense of danger, violation, and/or impasse. Disconnections may be acute, chronic, or traumatic.

DISCREPANT RELATIONAL IMAGES   Relational images that contradict the negative dominant and fixed images that keep people locked in disconnection; expansion of these images leads to changes in the dominant relational expectation.

EMPATHY   A complex affective-cognitive skill that allows us to "know" (resonate, feel, sense, cognitively grasp) another person's experience. For empathy to stimulate growth, the person usually thought of as the one being empathized with must see, know, and feel the empathy of the other. That is, she or he must see her or his impact on the other; this mutual empathy decreases the experience of isolation.

FIVE GOOD THINGS   Attributes of a growth-fostering relationship—zest, sense of worth, clarity, productivity, and a desire for more connection—as proposed by Jean Baker Miller.

FLUID EXPERTISE   Honoring the idea that both people bring wisdom and knowledge to an exchange; this supports the notion of mutual growth and respect.

GROWTH-FOSTERING RELATIONSHIP   A fundamental and complex process of active participation in the development and growth of other people and the relationship that results in mutual development (Miller & Stiver, 1997); such a relationship creates growth in both (or more) people.

HARDWIRED TO CONNECT   We now have abundant data that there is a biological basis for humans' need for connection. Modern neuroscience with its sophisticated technology shows us the ways that the brain grows in connection. We come into the world ready to connect, and disconnection, isolation, and exclusion create real pain. We need relationships just as we need air, water, and food, and we need them throughout our lives. We are ultimately interdependent beings. Our dilemma is that we are biologically programed to connect and flourish in relationships, but we live in a culture that eschews dependency and socializes us to be independent and autonomous. Our neurobiology clashes with our societal values and expectations; this creates considerable stress for all people.

HONORING STRATEGIES OF DISCONNECTION   Empathizing with an individual's strategies for avoiding connection, which includes being sensitive to her or his need for these strategies and the terror of being without them. These strategies are ways of staying out of connection because the only relationship that had been available was, in some fundamental way, disconnecting and violating; in other words, there was a good reason to develop the strategies (Miller & Stiver, 1997).

LOSS OF EMPATHIC POSSIBILITY   Feeling that others cannot possibly be empathic, losing even the capacity for self-empathy; one feels unworthy of connection, flawed in some essential way, which is often experienced in shame.

MUTUAL EMPATHY   Openness to being affected by and affecting another person. In mutual empathy, both people move with a sense of mutual respect, an intention for mutual growth, and an increasing capacity for connectedness. For mutual empathy to lead to growth, both people must see, know, and feel that they are being responded to, having an impact, and mattering to one another. The growth that occurs is both affective and cognitive and leads to an enlarged sense of community. Supported vulnerability, a feeling that one's vulnerability will not be taken advantage of or violated, is necessary for mutual empathy.

MUTUAL EMPOWERMENT   Along with mutual empathy, this term suggests that both people in any growth-fostering relationship are experiencing more aliveness, more clarity, and a greater sense of possibility and potential agency. Mutual empowerment is built on a relationship of "engagement," of being present and caring about the relationship as well as the individuals in it. It is a two-way (or more) dynamic process that functions as a central component of psychological growth, enhancing the strength of each individual in a relationship and ultimately creating strength in the larger community.

MUTUAL IMPACT   When each person feels that she or he is having an impact on each other and on the relationship; a shared power paradigm.

MUTUALITY   The concept in RCT suggesting that we grow toward an increased capacity for respect, having an impact on the other, and being open to being changed by the other. Jean Baker Miller's claim that if in a relationship both people are not growing, neither person is growing has been a controversial concept because some have critiqued RCT as encouraging the client to take care of the professional. RCT fully recognizes the responsibility of the clinician to pay attention to the growth of the client and not to invite caretaking from the client. But if the therapist does not open herself or himself to some impact and change (vulnerability), real growth will probably not occur for the client. Mutuality does not mean sameness, equality, or reciprocity; it is a way of relating, a shared activity in which each (or all) of the people involved are participating as fully as possible (Miller & Stiver, 1997).

POWER   Most fundamentally, the "capacity to produce a change" (Miller, 1986, p. 198).

POWER OVER   A concept in many societies that people can only feel safe and productive if they exercise power over others, keeping the others in a less advantaged position. The dominant group exercises power over other groups and individuals and does not encourage mutually empowering relationships. This model leads to disconnections and violations of relationships.

POWER WITH   Concept that more can be accomplished through collaborative efforts than through hierarchical arrangements, building on the notion that creativity and action develop in good connections. "Power with" grows as it empowers others and stands in opposition to "power over," which accrues through directing and controlling others.

PRIVILEGE   A system of advantage gained through another's disadvantage (McIntosh, 1980, 1988). Unearned privilege is accrued through an accident of birth or luck, being part of a privileged group. The myth of meritocracy sometimes makes it seem as if the advantage or privilege has been earned. For example, *White privilege* is "an invisible package of unearned assets that [a White person] can count on cashing in each day but about which [he or she] was 'meant' to remain oblivious" (McIntosh, 1988).

RACIAL IDENTITY DEVELOPMENT   Defined by Tatum (1993) as "a process of moving from internalized racism to a position of empowerment based on a positively affirmed sense of racial identity" (p. 3).

RACISM   Defined by Tatum (1993) as "a pervasive system of advantage based on race which has personal, cultural and institutional implications for our daily lives" (p. 2).

RADICAL RESPECT A deep appreciation based on empathy for the other person's current functioning and for the context within which her or his suffering arose; an equally deep appreciation for her or his coping methods, survival strategies, and the inner wisdom that sought to keep her or him alive.

RELATIONAL AWARENESS Being attentive to one's own experience, the other person, and the relationship and developing clarity about the movement of relationship.

RELATIONAL COMPETENCE The experience that one can be effective and have a positive impact on relationships; one feels that one matters and that one is responded to in a way that is empathic and open to mutual effect. Relational competence involves movement toward mutuality, developing anticipatory empathy, being open to being influenced, experiencing vulnerability as an inevitable place of potential growth rather than danger, and creating good connections rather than exercising power over others as the path of growth.

RELATIONAL CONFIDENCE Having confidence in a relationship and in the ability to contribute to growth-fostering relationships, as well as trust that others will join in creating such relationships.

RELATIONAL–CULTURAL MINDFULNESS Bringing attention to the other person, one's own responsiveness, the relationship, and the cultural context; being present with the energy and full movement of the relationship; feeling curiosity about the flow of the connection; letting go of images of how the interaction should be to discover what is; and awareness of one's own contributions to the quality of connection and disconnection in the relationship.

RELATIONAL EMPOWERMENT Shared sense of effectiveness, ability to act on the relationship, and moving toward connection. The relationship itself is strengthened and expanded in the movement of mutual empathy. Both (all) people in the interaction feel stronger, more alive, more able to create, and desirous of bringing this feeling of empowerment to others. This also contributes to productivity and creativity in the world.

RELATIONAL IMAGES   Inner pictures of what has happened to us in relationships, formed in important early relationships. As we develop these images, we are also creating a set of beliefs about why relationships are the way they are. Relational images thus determine expectations not only about what will occur in relationships but about a person's whole sense of herself or himself. They often become the unconscious frameworks by which we determine who we are, what we can do, and how worthwhile we are. Negative relational images become the source of a sense of lack of relational competence and worth and often support strategies of disconnection and a sense of hopelessness.

RELATIONAL MOVEMENT   Relationships are always in movement, toward either better connection or increasing disconnection; with an ongoing flow of mutual empathy, the participants move toward more connection.

RELATIONAL RESILIENCE   Movement to a mutually empowering, growth-fostering connection in the face of adverse conditions, traumatic experiences, and alienating sociocultural pressures; the ability to connect, reconnect, and/or resist disconnection. Movement toward empathic mutuality is at the core of relational resilience (Jordan, 1992).

SELF-EMPATHY   The ability to bring an empathic attitude to bear on one's own experience. Sometimes achieving self-empathy involves invoking an image of the client at an earlier age to reduce the self-blame and self-rejection that the individual carries.

SHAME   Pathological shame arises when one feels that one is no longer worthy of empathy or love. It shares many of the characteristics of condemned isolation. One feels excluded, unworthy, and beyond empathic possibility and that one cannot bring oneself more fully into relationship.

STRATEGIES OF DISCONNECTION   Methods people develop to stay out of relationship to prevent wounding or violation. Also known as *strategies of survival*, these evolve out of a person's attempt to find some way to make or preserve whatever connection is possible.

TRAUMATIC DISCONNECTION   Disconnections that occur when what might be an acute disconnection triggers someone (often suffering from posttraumatic stress disorder) into a place of reactivity (the amygdala hijack) where she or he becomes unavailable to relational repair. The person cannot come back into connection because of a heightened sense of danger. Until safety can be reestablished, the therapist must honor the client's dramatic return to strategies of disconnection. Ironically these traumatic disconnections sometimes follow an increase in closeness, a relinquishing of strategies of disconnection. In those moments, the client feels increased vulnerability and may have to resort to old ways of self-protection.

Suggested Readings

Banks, A. (2016). *Wired to connect: The surprising link between brain science and strong healthy relationships.* New York, NY: TarcherPerigee.

Collins, P. H. (2000). *Black feminist thought, knowledge, consciousness and the politics of empowerment* (2nd ed.). New York, NY: Routledge.

Comstock, D. L. (Ed.). (2005). *Diversity and development: Critical contexts that shape our lives and relationships.* Belmont, CA: Brooks/Cole, Cengage Learning.

Gilligan, C. (1982). *In a different voice.* Cambridge, MA: Harvard University Press.

Jordan, J. V. (Ed.). (1997). *Women's growth in diversity.* New York, NY: Guilford Press.

Jordan, J. V. (Ed.). (2010). *The power of connection: Recent developments in relational-cultural theory.* New York, NY: Routledge.

Jordan, J. V., & Carlson, J. (Eds.). (2013). *Creating connection: A relational-cultural approach with couples.* New York, NY: Routledge.

Jordan, J. V., Kaplan, A., Miller, J. B., Stiver, I., & Surrey, J. (1991). *Women's growth in connection.* New York, NY: Guilford Press.

Jordan, J. V., Walker, M., & Hartling, L. M. (Eds.). (2004). *The complexity of connection.* New York, NY: Guilford Press.

Miller, J. B. (1986). *Toward a new psychology of women.* Boston, MA: Beacon Press.

Miller, J. B., & Stiver, I. (1997). *The healing connection.* Boston, MA: Beacon Press.

Robb, C. (2006). *This changes everything: The relational revolution in psychology.* New York, NY: Farrar Strauss.

Shem, S., & Surrey, J. (1998). *We have to talk: Healing dialogues between women and men.* New York, NY: Basic Books.

Slater, L., Daniels, J., & Banks, A. (2004). *The complete guide to mental health for women.* Boston, MA: Beacon Press.

Walker, M., & Rosen, W. (2004). *How connections heal.* New York, NY: Guilford Press.

References

Alvarez, A. R., & Lazzari, M. M. (2016). Feminist mentoring and relational cultural theory: A case example and implications. *Affilia: Journal of Women & Social Work, 31*, 41–54. http://dx.doi.org/10.1177/0886109915612512

Alvarez, M. (1995). *The experience of migration: A relational approach in therapy* (Work in Progress No. 71). Wellesley, MA: Stone Center for Developmental Services and Studies, Wellesley College.

American Psychiatric Association. (2013). *Diagnostic and statistical manual of mental disorders* (5th ed.). Arlington, VA: Author.

Armstrong, M. (2008). Foundations for a gender based treatment model for women in recovery from chemical dependency. *Journal of Addictions Nursing, 19*, 77–82. http://dx.doi.org/10.1080/10884600802111663

Aron, L. (1996). *A meeting of minds: Mutuality in psychoanalysis.* New York, NY: Analytic Press.

Auslander, B. A., Perfect, M. M., Succop, P. A., & Rosenthal, S. L. (2007). Perceptions of sexual assertiveness among adolescent girls: Initiation, refusal, and use of protective behaviors. *Journal of Pediatric and Adolescent Gynecology, 20*, 157–162. http://dx.doi.org/10.1016/j.jpag.2007.03.093

Ayvazian, A., & Tatum, B. (1994). *Women, race and racism: A dialogue in black and white* (Work in Progress No. 68). Wellesley, MA: Stone Center for Developmental Services and Studies, Wellesley College.

Banks, A. (2000). *PTSD: Post-traumatic stress disorder: Relationship and brain chemistry* (Project Report No. 8). Wellesley, MA: Stone Center for Developmental Services and Studies, Wellesley College.

Banks, A. (2005). The developmental impact of trauma. In D. Comstock (Ed.), *Diversity and development: Critical contexts that shape our lives and relationships* (pp. 185–213). Belmont, CA: Brooks/Cole.

Banks, A. (2006a). *The neurobiology of connection*. Wellesley, MA: Presentation at Summer Training Institute, Jean Baker Miller Training Institute.

Banks, A. (2006b). Relational therapy for trauma. *Journal of Psychological Trauma, 5*, 25–47.

Banks, A. (2011). Developing the capacity to connect. *Zygon, 46*, 168–182. http://dx.doi.org/10.1111/j.1467-9744.2010.01164.x

Banks, A. (2016). *Wired to connect*. New York, NY: Tarcher/Penguin.

Barnett, R., & Rivers, C. (2004). *Same difference: How gender myths are hurting our relationships, our children and our jobs*. New York, NY: Basic Books.

Beesley, D., & Frey, L. (2008). Conducting groups in schools: Challenges and reward. In H. Coleman & C. Yeh (Eds.), *Handbook on school counseling* (pp. 431–447). New York, NY: Erlbaum.

Begley, S. (2008). *Train your mind, change your brain*. New York, NY: Ballantine Books.

Bekteshi, V., & Kayser, K. (2013). When a mother has cancer: Pathways to relational growth for mothers and daughters coping with cancer. *Psycho-Oncology, 22*, 2379–2385.

Belenky, M., Clinchy, B., Goldberger, N., & Tarule, J. (1986). *Women's ways of knowing*. New York, NY: Basic Books.

Belford, B., Kaehler, L. A., & Birrell, P. (2012). Relational health as a mediator between betrayal trauma and borderline personality disorder. *Journal of Trauma & Dissociation, 13*, 244–257. http://dx.doi.org/10.1080/15299732.2012.642750

Bell, P. W. (2008). *The relational patterns between African American mothers under correctional supervision and maternal caregiving grandmothers* (Doctoral dissertation). Retrieved from ProQuest Dissertations & Theses Gradworks website: http://gradworks.umi.com/33/09/3309004.html

Bergman, S. J. (1991). *Men's psychological development: A relational perspective* (Work in Progress No. 48). Wellesley, MA: Stone Center for Developmental Services and Studies, Wellesley College.

Bergman, S. J. (1996). Male relational dread. *Psychiatric Annals, 26*, 24–28. http://dx.doi.org/10.3928/0048-5713-19960101-08

Bergman, S. J., & Surrey, J. (1994). *Couple therapy: A relational approach* (Work in Progress No. 66). Wellesley, MA: Stone Center for Developmental Services and Studies, Wellesley College.

Bergman, S. J., & Surrey, J. (2013). An interview with Stephen Bergman and Janet Surrey. In J. V. Jordan & J. Carlson (Eds.), *Creating connection: A relational-cultural approach with couples* (pp. 11–22). New York, NY: Routledge.

Beyene, T., Anglin, M., Sanchez, W., & Ballou, M. (2002). Mentoring and relational mutuality: Protégés' perspectives. *Journal of Humanistic Counseling, 41*, 87–102. http://dx.doi.org/10.1002/j.2164-490X.2002.tb00132.x

Birrell, P. J. (2006). Ethics of possibility: Relationship, risk and presence. *Ethics & Behavior, 16*, 95–115. http://dx.doi.org/10.1207/s15327019eb1602_2

Birrell, P. J., & Bruns, C. M. (2016). Ethics and relationship: From risk management to relational engagement. *Journal of Counseling & Development, 94*, 391–397. http://dx.doi.org/10.1002/jcad.12097

Birrell, P. J., & Freyd, J. J. (2006). Betrayal trauma: Relational models of harm and healing. *Journal of Psychological Trauma, 5*, 49–52.

Boatwright, K. J., & Nolan, B. B. (2006). Growthful connections: Relational-cultural theory in therapeutic action. *Psychology of Women Quarterly, 30*, 232. http://dx.doi.org/10.1111/j.1471-6402.2006.00285_2.x

Brimm, L. (2010). *Global cosmopolitans. The creative edge of difference.* New York, NY: Palgrave Macmillan. http://dx.doi.org/10.1057/9780230289796

Brown, L. M. (1998). *Raising their voices: The politics of girls' anger.* Cambridge, MA: Harvard University Press.

Brown, L. M., & Gilligan, C. (1992). *Meeting at the crossroads: Women's psychology and girls' development.* Cambridge, MA: Harvard University Press. http://dx.doi.org/10.4159/harvard.9780674731837

Brown, L. S., & Ballou, M. (Eds.). (2002). *Rethinking mental health and disorder: Feminist perspectives.* New York, NY: Guilford Press.

Brown, N. M. (2010). *Early adolescent girls in the middle school environment: Enhancing self esteem through relational development* (Doctoral dissertation). Retrieved from ProQuest Information & Learning. (Publication 340517)

Brubaker, L. (2010). Growth through interdependence. *PsycCRITIQUES, 55*(46).

Bures, F. (2007, October). Free your mind. *Madison Magazine.* Retrieved from http://www.channel3000.com/madison-magazine/city-life/free-your-mind/162400186

Cannon, K. B. (2007). *Increasing relational capacities utilizing relational practice groups in a population of relationally aggressive adolescent females* (Unpublished doctoral dissertation). St. Mary's University, San Antonio, TX.

Cannon, K. B., Hammer, T. R., Reicherzer, S., & Gilliam, B. J. (2012). Relational-cultural theory: A framework for relational competence and movement in group work with female adolescents. *Journal of Creativity in Mental Health, 7*, 2–16. http://dx.doi.org/10.1080/15401383.2012.660118

Cannon, K. B., Patton, L., & Reicherzer, S. L. (2014). Relational cultural theory in the context of feminism. In R. D. Parsons & N. Zhang (Eds.), *Counseling theory: Guiding reflective practice* (pp. 343–369). Thousand Oaks, CA: Sage. http://dx.doi.org/10.4135/9781483399621.n13

Caplan, P., & Cosgrove, L. (2004). *Bias in psychiatric diagnosis.* New York, NY: Aronson.

Carter, E., & McGoldrick, M. (2005). *The expanded family life cycle: Individual, family and social perspectives* (3rd ed.). Boston, MA: Allyn & Bacon.

Carter, T. J. (2012). In hope of transformation: Teaching and learning through relational practice in the adult learning classroom. In C. J. Boden McGill & S. M. Kippers (Eds.), *Best pathways to transformation: Learning in relationship* (pp. 83–96). Charlotte, NC: Information Age.

Chhabra, M. (2006). *Finding voice: Exploring possibilities of healing in conversations on an event of collective mass violence between self and other—An interaction between Indian and Pakistani youth on the 1947 partition* (Unpublished doctoral dissertation). Leslie University, Cambridge, MA.

Cholewa, B., Goodman, R. D., West-Olatunji, C., & Amatea, E. (2014). A qualitative examination of the impact of culturally responsive educational practices on the psychological well-being of students of color. *The Urban Review, 46,* 574–596. http://dx.doi.org/10.1007/s11256-014-0272-y

Chugani, H. T., Behen, M. E., Muzik, O., Juhász, C., Nagy, F., & Chugani, D. C. (2001). Local brain functional activity following early deprivation: A study of postinstitutionalized Romanian orphans. *NeuroImage, 14,* 1290–1301. http://dx.doi.org/10.1006/nimg.2001.0917

Coates, T.-N. (2015). *Between the world and me.* New York, NY: Spiegel & Grau.

Coll, C., Cook-Nobles, R., & Surrey, J. (1995). *Building connection through diversity* (Work in Progress No. 64). Wellesley, MA: Stone Center for Developmental Services and Studies, Wellesley College.

Coll, C., & Duff, K. (1995). *Reframing the needs of women in prison: A relational and diversity perspective* (Project Report No. 4). Wellesley, MA: Stone Center for Developmental Services and Studies, Wellesley College.

Collins, P. H. (1990). *Black feminist thought: Knowledge, consciousness and the politics of empowerment.* Boston, MA: Unwin Hyman.

Collins, P. H. (2000). *Black feminist thought* (2nd ed.). New York, NY: Routledge.

Comas-Diaz, L., & Weiner, M. B. (2013). Sisters of the heart: How women's friendships heal. *Women & Therapy, 36,* 1–10. http://dx.doi.org/10.1080/02703149.2012.720199

Comstock, D. (Ed.). (2005). *Diversity and development: Critical contexts that shape our lives and relationships.* Belmont, CA: Brooks/Cole.

Comstock, D., Hammer, T. R., Strentzsch, J., Cannon, K., Parsons, J., & Salazar, G. (2008). Relational-cultural theory: A framework for bridging relational, multicultural and social justice competencies. *Journal of Counseling & Development, 86,* 279–287. http://dx.doi.org/10.1002/j.1556-6678.2008.tb00510.x

Comstock-Benzick, D. L. (2013). A relational-cultural perspective of divorce. In J. V. Jordan & J. Carlson (Eds.), *Creating connection: A relational-cultural approach with couples* (pp. 205–224). New York, NY: Routledge.

Cooley, C. (1968). The social self: On the meanings of "I." In C. Gordon & K. Gergen (Eds.), *The self in social interaction* (pp. 87–93). New York, NY: Wiley. (Original work published 1902)

Corey, G. (2009). *Theory and practice of counseling and psychotherapy* (8th ed.). Belmont, CA: Thomson.

Covington, S. S. (1994). *A woman's way through the twelve steps*. Center City, MN: Hazelden.

Covington, S. S. (1999). *Helping women recover: A program for treating addiction*. San Francisco, CA: Jossey-Bass.

Covington, S. S. (2008). Women and addiction: A trauma-informed approach. *Journal of Psychoactive Drugs, 40*(Suppl. 5), 377–385. http://dx.doi.org/ 10.1080/02791072.2008.10400665

Covington, S. S., & Surrey, J. (2000). *The relational model of women's psychological development: Implications for substance abuse* (Work in Progress No. 91). Wellesley, MA: Stone Center for Developmental Services and Studies, Wellesley College.

Cozolino, L. (2014). *The neuroscience of human relationships: Attachment and the developing social brain* (2nd ed.). New York, NY: Norton.

Davanloo, H. (Ed.). (1980). *Short-term dynamic psychotherapy*. New York, NY: Aronson.

Deanow, C. G. (2011). Relational development through the life cycle: Capacities, opportunities, challenges and obstacles. *Affilia, 26*, 125–138. http:// dx.doi.org/10.1177/0886109911405485

Desai, L. (1999). *Relational theory in a South Asian context: An example of the dynamics of identity development* (Work in Progress No 86). Wellesley, MA: Stone Center for Developmental Services and Studies, Wellesley College.

Doidge, N. (2007). *The brain that changes itself*. New York, NY: Viking.

Dooley, C. (2000). Culture and the development of eating disorders in women. In J. Jordan & C. Dooley (Eds.), *Relational practice in action* (Project Report No. 6). Wellesley, MA: Stone Center Working Papers Series, Wellesley College.

Dooley, C., & Fedele, N. (1999). *Mothers and sons: Raising relational boys* (Work in Progress No. 84). Wellesley, MA: Stone Center Working Paper Series, Wellesley College.

Downs, M. (2006). *Between us: Growing relational possibilities in clinical supervision* (Work in Progress No. 105). Wellesley, MA: Stone Center for Developmental Services and Studies, Wellesley College.

Downs, M. (2012). Changing the meaning of help: Clinical approaches to reducing stigma among suicidal young adults. *Families in Society, 93*, 22–28. http://dx.doi.org/10.1606/1044-3894.4182

Dubus, N. (2014). Permission to be authentic: An intervention for postpartum women. *Affilia: Journal of Women and Social Work, 29*, 43–55. http://dx.doi.org/10.1177/0886109913509539

Duffey, T. (2006). Grief, loss and death. In D. Comstock (Ed.), *Diversity and development: Critical contexts that shape our lives and relationships* (pp. 253–268). Belmont, CA: Brooks/Cole.

Duffey, T., & Haberstroh, S. (2012). Female counselors working with male clients using relational cultural theory. In M. Englar-Carlson & M. P. Evans, *A counselor's guide to working with men* (pp. 307–324). Alexandria, VA: American Counseling Association.

Duffey, T., & Haberstroh, S. (2014). Developmental relational counseling: Applications for counseling men. *Journal of Counseling & Development, 92*, 104–113. http://dx.doi.org/10.1002/j.1556-6676.2014.00136.x

Duffey, T., & Somody, C. (2011). The role of relational-cultural theory in mental health counseling. *Journal of Mental Health Counseling, 33*, 223–242. http://dx.doi.org/10.17744/mehc.33.3.c10410226u275647

Duffey, T., & Trepal, H. (2016). Introduction to the special section on relational-cultural theory. *Journal of Counseling & Development, 94*, 379–382. http://dx.doi.org/10.1002/jcad.12095

Edwards, J. B., Bryant, S., & Clark, I. T. (2008). African American female social work educators in predominantly white schools of social work: Strategies for thriving. *Journal of African American Studies, 12*, 37–49. http://dx.doi.org/10.1007/s12111-007-9029-y

Edwards, J. B., Gomes, M., & Major, M. A. (2013). The charged economic environment: Its role in parental psychological distress and development of children, adolescents, and young adults. *Journal of Human Behavior in the Social Environment, 23*, 256–266. http://dx.doi.org/10.1080/10911359.2013.747350

Eisenberger, N. I., & Lieberman, M. D. (2004). Why rejection hurts: A common neural alarm system for physical and social pain. *Trends in Cognitive Sciences, 8*, 294–300. http://dx.doi.org/10.1016/j.tics.2004.05.010

Eisenberger, N. I., & Lieberman, M. D. (2005). Why it hurts to be left out: The neurocognitive overlap between physical and social pain. In K. D. Williams, J. P. Forgas, & W. von Hippel (Eds.), *The social outcast: Ostracism, social exclusion, rejection and bullying* (pp. 109–127). New York, NY: Cambridge University Press.

Eisenberger, N. I., Lieberman, M. D., & Williams, K. D. (2003). Does rejection hurt? An fMRI study of social exclusion. *Science, 302*, 290–292. http://dx.doi.org/10.1126/science.1089134

Eldridge, N. S. (2013). Supporting relational growth in a shifting cultural environment: Therapy with lesbian couples. In J. V. Jordan & J. Carlson (Eds.), *Creating connection: A relational-cultural approach with couples* (pp. 75–90). New York, NY: Routledge.

Eldridge, N. S., Mencher, J., & Slater, S. (1993). *The conundrum of mutuality: A lesbian dialogue* (Work in Progress No. 62). Wellesley, MA: Stone Center for Developmental Services and Studies, Wellesley College.

Eldridge, N. S., Surrey, J. L., Rosen, W. P., & Miller, J. B. (2008). So what changes in therapy? *Women & Therapy, 31,* 31–50. http://dx.doi.org/10.1080/02703140802145763

Emerson, A. M., & Ramaswamy, M. (2015). Theories and assumptions that inform trauma-specific interventions for incarcerated women. *Family & Community Health, 38,* 240–251. http://dx.doi.org/10.1097/FCH.0000000000000073

Englar-Carlson, M., Evans, M. P., & Duffey, T. A. (2014). *A counselor's guide to working with men.* Alexandria, VA: American Counseling Association.

Englar-Carlson, M., Stevens, M. A., & Scholz, R. (2010). *Psychotherapy with men.* New York, NY: Springer. http://dx.doi.org/10.1007/978-1-4419-1467-5_10

Engler, B. (2003). *Personality theories: An introduction* (6th ed.). Boston, MA: Houghton Mifflin.

Engler, B. (2006). *Personality theories: An introduction* (7th ed.). Boston, MA: Houghton Mifflin.

Etienne, T. R. (2011). *The evolution of the African American mother–daughter relationship: A grounded theory study* (Doctoral dissertation). Retrieved from Walden University ScholarWorks: http://scholarworks.waldenu.edu/dissertations/1072

Fairbairn, W. (1962). *Object relations and dynamic structure: In an object relations theory of personality.* New York, NY: Basic Books. (Original work published 1959)

Fedele, N. (2004). Relationship in groups: Connection, resonance, and paradox. In J. Jordan, M. Walker, & L. Hartling (Eds.), *The complexity of connection: Writings from the Stone Center's Jean Baker Miller Training Institute* (pp. 194–219). New York, NY: Guilford Press.

Finkelstein, N. (1996). Using the relational model in a context for treating pregnant and parenting chemically dependent women. In B. L. Underhill & D. G. Finnegan (Eds.), *Chemical dependency: Women at risk* (pp. 23–44). New York, NY: Haworth. http://dx.doi.org/10.1300/J034v06n01_02

Fishbane, M. D. (2013). A neurobiological-relational approach to couple therapy. In J. V. Jordan & J. Carlson (Eds.), *Creating connection: A relational-cultural approach with couples* (pp. 166–185). New York, NY: Routledge.

Fletcher, J. K. (1999). *Disappearing acts: Gender, power and relational practice at work.* Cambridge, MA: MIT Press.

Fletcher, J. K. (2004). Relational theory in the workplace. In J. V. Jordan, M. Walker, & L. M. Hartling (Eds.), *The complexity of connection: Writing from the Stone Center's Jean Baker Miller Training Institute* (pp. 270–298). New York, NY: Guilford Press.

Fletcher, J. K. (2007). Leadership, power, and positive relationships. In J. E. Dutton & B. R. Ragins (Eds.), *Exploring positive relationships at work: Building theoretical and research foundations* (pp. 347–371). Mahwah, NJ: Erlbaum.

Fletcher, J. K. (2012). The relational practice of leadership. In M. Uhl-Bien & S. M. Ospina (Eds.), *Advancing relational leadership research: A dialogue among perspectives* (pp. 83–106). Charlotte, NC: IIAP Information Age.

Fletcher, J. K., Jordan, J. V., & Miller, J. B. (2000). Women and the workplace: Applications of a psychodynamic theory. *The American Journal of Psychoanalysis, 60*, 243–261. http://dx.doi.org/10.1023/A:1001973704517

Frager, R., & Fadiman, J. (Eds.). (1998). *Personality and personal growth* (4th ed.). New York, NY: Addison Wesley Longman.

Frager, R., & Fadiman, J. (2013). *Personality and personal growth* (7th ed.). New York, NY: Pearson.

Frederickson, B. (2013). *Love 2.0.* New York, NY: Plume.

Freedberg, S. (2007). Re-examining empathy: A relational–feminist point of view. *Social Work, 52*, 251–259. http://dx.doi.org/10.1093/sw/52.3.251

Freud, S. (1955). Beyond the pleasure principle. In J. Strachey (Ed.), *The standard edition of the complete psychological works of Sigmund Freud* (Vol. 18, pp. 3–64). London, England: Hogarth Press. (Original work published 1920)

Freud, S. (1957). The future prospects of psychoanalytic therapy. In J. Strachey (Ed.), *The standard edition of the complete psychological works of Sigmund Freud* (Vol. 2, pp. 139–152). London, England: Hogarth Press.

Freud, S. (1958). Recommendations to physicians practicing psychoanalysis. In J. Strachey (Ed.), *The standard edition of the complete psychological works of Sigmund Freud* (Vol. 12, pp. 111–120). London, England: Hogarth Press. (Original work published 1912)

Frew, J., & Spiegler, M. D. (2012). *Contemporary psychotherapies for a diverse world* (1st Rev. Ed.). New York, NY: Routledge.

Frey, L. L. (2013). Relational-cultural therapy: Theory, research and application to counseling competencies. *Professional Psychology: Research and Practice, 44*, 177–185. http://dx.doi.org/10.1037/a0033121

Frey, L. L., Beesley, D., Hurst, R., Saldana, S., & Licuanan, B. (2016). Instrumentality, expressivity and relational qualities in same sex friendships of college women and men. *Journal of College Counseling, 19*, 17–30. http://dx.doi.org/10.1002/jocc.12028

Frey, L. L., Beesley, D., & Miller, J. B. (2006). Relational health attachment and psychological distress in college women and men. *Psychology of Women Quarterly, 30,* 303–311. http://dx.doi.org/10.1111/j.1471-6402.2006.00298.x

Frey, L. L., Beesley, D., & Newman, J. (2005). The relational health indices: Reanalysis of a measure of relational quality. *Measurement and Evaluation in Counseling & Development, 38,* 153–163.

Frey, L. L., & Melrath-Dyer, E. (2005). Sexually coercive behavior of male adolescents toward peers and adults: A relational perspective. In R. Longo & D. Prescott (Eds.), *Current perspective: Working with aggressive youth and youths with sexual behavior problems* (pp. 235–254). Holyoke, MA: NEARI Press.

Frey, L. L., Tobin, J., & Beesley, D. (2004). Relational predictors of psychological distress in women and men presenting for university counseling center services. *Journal of College Counseling, 7,* 129–139. http://dx.doi.org/10.1002/j.2161-1882.2004.tb00244.x

Genero, N., Miller, J. B., & Surrey, J. (1992). *The mutual psychological development questionnaire* (Project Report No. 1). Wellesley, MA: Stone Center for Developmental Services and Studies, Wellesley College.

Genero, N., Miller, J. B., Surrey, J., & Baldwin, L. (1992). Measuring perceived mutuality in close relationship: Validation of the mutual psychological development questionnaire. *Journal of Family Psychology, 6,* 36–48. http://dx.doi.org/10.1037/0893-3200.6.1.36

Gerlock, A. A. (2001). A profile of who completes and who drops out of domestic violence rehabilitation. *Issues in Mental Health Nursing, 22,* 379–400. http://dx.doi.org/10.1080/01612840116997

Gerlock, A. A. (2004). Domestic violence and post-traumatic stress disorder severity for participants of a domestic violence rehabilitation program. *Military Medicine, 169,* 470–474. http://dx.doi.org/10.7205/MILMED.169.6.470

Germer, C. (2009). *The mindful path to self compassion: Freeing yourself from destructive thoughts and emotions.* New York, NY: Guilford Press.

Gibson, D. M. (2007). The relationship of infertility and death: Using the relational/cultural model of counseling in making meaning. *The Humanistic Psychologist, 35,* 275–289. http://dx.doi.org/10.1080/08873260701415348

Gibson, D. M., & Myers, J. E. (2002). The effect of social coping resources and growth-fostering relationships on infertility stress in women. *Journal of Mental Health Counseling, 24,* 68–80.

Gill, M. D. (1983). *Analysis of transference* (Vol. I). New York, NY: International Universities Press.

Gilligan, C. (1982). *In a different voice.* Cambridge, MA: Harvard University Press.

Gilligan, C. (1990). Joining the resistance: Psychology, politics, girls and women. *Michigan Quarterly Review, 29,* 501–536.

Gilligan, C., Lyons, N., & Hanmer, T. (1990). *Making connections: The relational worlds of adolescent girls at Emma Willard School.* Cambridge, MA: Harvard University Press.

Gilligan, C., Rogers, A., & Tolman, D. (Eds.). (1991). *Women, girls and psychotherapy: Reframing resistance.* Binghamton, NY: Haworth Press.

Goleman, D. (1997). *Emotional intelligence.* New York, NY: Bantam Books.

Goleman, D. (2006). *Social intelligence: The new science of human relationships.* New York, NY: Bantam Books.

Gómez, J. M., Lewis, J. K., Noll, L. K., Smidt, A. M., & Birrell, P. J. (2016). Shifting the focus: Nonpathologizing approaches to healing from betrayal trauma through an emphasis on relational care. *Journal of Trauma & Dissociation, 17,* 165–185. http://dx.doi.org/10.1080/15299732.2016.1103104

Greene, B. (1990). What has gone before: The legacy of racism and sexism in the lives of black mothers and daughters. *Women & Therapy, 9,* 207–230. http://dx.doi.org/10.1300/J015v09n01_12

Grepmair, L., Mitterlehner, F., Loew, T., Bachler, E., Rother, W., & Nickel, M. (2007). Promoting mindfulness in psychotherapists in training influences the treatment results of their patients: A randomized, double-blind, controlled study. *Psychotherapy and Psychosomatics, 76,* 332–338. http://dx.doi.org/10.1159/000107560

Gu, Q., & Day, C. (2007). Teachers resilience: A necessary condition for effectiveness. *Teaching and Teacher Education, 23,* 1302–1316. http://dx.doi.org/10.1016/j.tate.2006.06.006

Guntrip, H. (1973). *Psychoanalytic theory, therapy and the self.* New York, NY: Basic Books.

Haley, J. (1997). *Leaving home: The therapy of disturbed young people.* New York, NY: Routledge.

Hartling, L. M. (1995). *Humiliation: Assessing the specter of derision, degradation, and debasement* (Unpublished doctoral dissertation). The Union Institute Graduate School, Cincinnati, OH.

Hartling, L. M. (2005). Fostering resilience throughout our lives: New relational possibilities. In D. Comstock (Ed.), *Diversity and development: Critical contexts that shape our lives and relationships* (pp. 337–354). Belmont, CA: Brooks/Cole.

Hartling, L. M. (2008). Strengthening resilience in a risky world: It's all about relationships. *Women & Therapy, 31,* 51–70. http://dx.doi.org/10.1080/02703140802145870

Hartling, L. M., & Lindner, E. (2016). Healing humiliation: From reaction to creative action. *Journal of Counseling & Development, 94*, 383–390. http://dx.doi.org/10.1002/jcad.12096

Hartling, L. M., & Luchetta, T. (1999). Humiliation: Assessing the impact of derision, degradation and debasement. *The Journal of Primary Prevention, 19*, 259–278. http://dx.doi.org/10.1023/A:1022622422521

Hartling, L. M., Rosen, W., Walker, M., & Jordan, J. V. (2000). *Shame and humiliation: From isolation to relational transformation* (Work in Progress No. 88). Wellesley, MA: Stone Center for Developmental Services and Studies, Wellesley College.

Hartling, L. M., & Sparks, L. (2008). Relational-cultural practice: Working in a nonrelational world. *Women & Therapy, 31*, 165–188. http://dx.doi.org/10.1080/02703140802146332

Headley, J. A., & Sangganjanavanich, V. F. (2014). A recipe for change: Promoting connection through relational-cultural theory. *Journal of Creativity in Mental Health, 9*, 245–261. http://dx.doi.org/10.1080/15401383.2013.879756

Heineman, C. J. (2003). *The relationship between perceived mutuality and attitudes of sexism, racism, and heterosexism: Searching for a common factor* (Unpublished doctoral dissertation). Ball State University, Muncie, IN.

Helms, J. E., & Cook, D. (1999). *Using race and culture in counseling and psychotherapy: Therapy and process.* Boston, MA: Allyn & Bacon.

Herman, J. (1992). *Trauma and recovery.* New York, NY: Basic Books.

Hoffman, M. L. (1977). Sex differences in empathy and related behaviors. *Psychological Bulletin, 84*, 712–722. http://dx.doi.org/10.1037/0033-2909.84.4.712

Hoffman, M. L. (1978). Towards a theory of empathic arousal and development. In M. Lewis & L. Rosenblum (Eds.), *The development of affect* (pp. 227–256). New York, NY: Plenum Press. http://dx.doi.org/10.1007/978-1-4684-2616-8_9

Hoffnung, M. (2005). No more blaming the victim: Therapy in the interest of social justice. *Psychology of Women Quarterly, 29*, 454–455.

hooks, b. (1984). *Feminist theory: From margin to center.* Boston, MA: South End Press.

Hossfeld, B. (2008). Developing friendships and peer relationships: Building social support with the Girls Circle Program. In C. W. LeCroy & J. E. Mann (Eds.), *Handbooks of prevention and intervention programs for adolescent girls* (pp. 42–80). Hoboken, NJ: Wiley.

Hutchison, W. D., Davis, K. D., Lozano, A. M., Tasker, R. R., & Dostrovsky, J. O. (1999). Pain-related neurons in the human cingulate cortex. *Nature Neuroscience, 2*, 403–405. http://dx.doi.org/10.1038/8065

Iacoboni, M. (2009). *Mirroring people: The science of empathy and how we connect with others*. New York, NY: Picador.

Ivey, A., D'Andrea, M., Ivey, M., & Simek-Morgan, L. (2007). *Theories of counseling and psychotherapy: A multicultural perspective*. New York, NY: Pearson.

Jack, D. (1991). *Silencing the self: Women and depression*. Cambridge, MA: Harvard University Press.

Jack, D. (1999). *Behind the mask: Destruction and creativity in women's aggression*. Cambridge, MA: Harvard University Press.

Jenkins, Y. (1993). Diversity and social esteem. In V. De La Cancela, J. Chin, & Y. Jenkins (Eds.), *Diversity in psychotherapy: The politics of race, ethnicity and gender* (pp. 45–64). Westport, CT: Praeger.

Jenkins, Y. (Ed.). (1998). *Diversity in college settings: Directives for helping professionals*. New York, NY: Routledge.

Johannessen, C. A. (2013). Healthy relationships during unhealthy times: Relational-cultural theory group for partners facing cancer. In J. V. Jordan & J. Carlson (Eds.), *Creating connection: A relational-cultural approach with couples* (pp. 186–204). New York, NY: Routledge.

Johnson, K., & Ferguson, T. (1990). *Trusting ourselves: The sourcebook on the psychology of women*. New York, NY: Atlantic Monthly Press.

Johnson, S. (2008). *Hold me tight: Seven conversations for a lifetime of love*. New York, NY: Little Brown.

Jordan, J. V. (1983). *Women and empathy* (Work in Progress No. 2). Wellesley, MA: Stone Center for Developmental Services and Studies, Wellesley College.

Jordan, J. V. (1986). *The meaning of mutuality* (Work in Progress No. 23). Wellesley, MA: Stone Center for Developmental Services and Studies, Wellesley College.

Jordan, J. V. (1989). *Relational development: Therapeutic implications of empathy and shame* (Work in Progress No. 39). Wellesley, MA: Stone Center for Developmental Services and Studies, Wellesley College.

Jordan, J. V. (1990). *Courage in connection: Conflict, compassion and creativity* (Work in Progress No. 45). Wellesley, MA: Stone Center for Developmental Services and Studies, Wellesley College.

Jordan, J. V. (1992). *Relational resilience* (Work in Progress No. 57). Wellesley, MA: Stone Center for Developmental Services and Studies, Wellesley College.

Jordan, J. V. (1995a). Boundaries: A relational perspective. *Psychotherapie Forum, 1,* 1–4.

Jordan, J. V. (1995b). *Relational awareness: Transforming disconnection* (Work in Progress No. 76). Wellesley, MA: Stone Center for Developmental Services and Studies, Wellesley College.

Jordan, J. V. (Ed.). (1997). *Women's growth in diversity*. New York, NY: Guilford Press.

Jordan, J. V. (1998). *Mothers and daughters, mothers and sons: Relational dilemmas and opportunities*. Invited Lecture, National Conference on Young People, New England Consultants, Braintree, MA.

Jordan, J. V. (1999). *Toward connection and competence* (Work in Progress No. 83). Wellesley, MA: Stone Center for Developmental Services and Studies, Wellesley College.

Jordan, J. V. (2000). The role of mutual empathy in relational/cultural therapy. *Journal of Clinical Psychology, 56*, 1005–1016. http://dx.doi.org/10.1002/1097-4679(200008)56:8<1005::AID-JCLP2>3.0.CO;2-L

Jordan, J. V. (2001). A relational-cultural model: Healing through mutual empathy. *Bulletin of the Menninger Clinic, 65*, 92–103. http://dx.doi.org/10.1521/bumc.65.1.92.18707

Jordan, J. V. (2002). A relational-cultural perspective in therapy. In F. Kazlow (Ed.), *Comprehensive handbook of psychotherapy* (Vol. 3, pp. 233–254). New York, NY: Wiley.

Jordan, J. V. (2003). Relational-cultural theory. In M. Kopala & M. Keitel (Eds.), *Handbook of counseling women* (pp. 22–30). Thousand Oaks, CA: Sage. http://dx.doi.org/10.4135/9781452229546.n2

Jordan, J. V. (2004). Personality disorder or relational disconnection? In J. Magnavita (Ed.), *Handbook of personality disorders: Theory and practice* (pp. 120–134). New York, NY: Wiley.

Jordan, J. V. (2006). Relational resilience in girls. In S. Goldstein & R. Brooks (Eds.), *Handbook of resilience in children* (pp. 79–90). New York, NY: Plenum.

Jordan, J. V. (2008a). Commitment to connection in a culture of fear. *Women & Therapy, 31*, 235–254. http://dx.doi.org/10.1080/02703140802146423

Jordan, J. V. (2008b). Learning at the margin: New models of strength. *Women & Therapy, 31*, 189–208. http://dx.doi.org/10.1080/02703140802146365

Jordan, J. V. (Ed.). (2008c). *The power of connection*. Philadelphia, PA: Haworth Press.

Jordan, J. V. (2008d). Recent developments in relational-cultural theory [Special issue]. *Women & Therapy, 31*(2–4). http://dx.doi.org/10.1080/02703140802145540

Jordan, J. V. (2008e). Valuing vulnerability: New definitions of courage. *Women & Therapy, 31*, 209–233. http://dx.doi.org/10.1080/02703140802146399

Jordan, J. V. (2009). Losing certainty and finding voice: One therapist's reflections on doing therapy in the last third of life. *Women & Therapy, 32*, 239–251. http://dx.doi.org/10.1080/02703140902851872

Jordan, J. V. (2010). *Relational–cultural therapy*. Washington, DC: American Psychological Association.

Jordan, J. V. (2011a). Disconnection and parenting: A relational–cultural perspective. In S. M. Dunham, S. B. Dormer, & J. Carlson (Eds.), *Poisonous parenting: Toxic relationships between parents and their adult children* (pp. 145–162). New York, NY: Routledge/Taylor & Francis Group.

Jordan, J. V. (2011b). The Stone Center and relational–cultural theory. In J. C. Norcross, G. R. VandenBos, & D. K. Freedheim (Eds.), *History of psychotherapy: Continuity and change* (2nd ed., pp. 357–369). Washington, DC: American Psychological Association. http://dx.doi.org/10.1037/12353-012

Jordan, J. V. (2013). Relational resilience in girls. In S. Goldstein & R. Brooks (Eds.), *Handbook of resilience in children* (2nd ed., pp. 73–86). New York, NY: Springer Science and Business Media. http://dx.doi.org/10.1007/978-1-4614-3661-4_5

Jordan, J. V. (2014). Relational–cultural therapy. In G. R. VandenBos, E. Meidenbauer, & J. Frank-McNeil (Eds.), *Psychotherapy theories and techniques: A reader* (pp. 325–333). Washington, DC: American Psychological Association. http://dx.doi.org/10.1037/14295-035

Jordan, J. V. (2017). Relational-cultural therapy. In M. Kopala & M. Keitel (Eds.), *Handbook of counseling women* (2nd ed., pp. 63–73). Thousand Oaks, CA: Sage.

Jordan, J. V., & Carlson, J. (Eds.). (2013). *Creating connection: A relational-cultural approach with couples.* New York, NY: Routledge.

Jordan, J. V., & Dooley, C. (2000). *Relational practice in action: A group manual* (Project Report No. 6). Wellesley, MA: Stone Center for Developmental Services and Studies, Wellesley College.

Jordan, J. V., Handel, M., Alvarez, M., & Cook-Noble, R. (2000). *Applications of the relational model to time limited therapy* (Work in Progress No. 87). Wellesley, MA: Stone Center for Developmental Services and Studies, Wellesley College.

Jordan, J. V., & Hartling, L. M. (2002). New developments in relational-cultural theory. In M. Ballou & L. Brown (Eds.), *Rethinking mental health and disorder: Feminist perspectives* (pp. 48–70). New York, NY: Guilford Press.

Jordan, J. V., Kaplan, A., Miller, J. B., Stiver, I., & Surrey, J. (1991). *Women's growth in connection.* New York, NY: Guilford Press.

Jordan, J. V., & Romney, P. (2005). Women in the workplace: An application of relational–cultural theory. In M. P. Mirkin, K. L. Suyemoto, & B. F. Okun (Eds.), *Psychotherapy with women: Exploring diverse contexts and identities* (pp. 198–214). New York, NY: Guilford Press.

Jordan, J. V., & Walker, M. (2004). Introduction. In J. V. Jordan, M. Walker, & L. M. Hartling (Eds.), *The complexity of connection: Writings from the Stone Center's Jean Baker Miller Training Institute* (pp. 1–8). New York, NY: Guilford Press.

Jordan, J. V., Walker, M., & Hartling, L. M. (Eds.). (2004). *The complexity of connection: Writings from the Stone Center's Jean Baker Miller Training Institute.* New York, NY: Guilford Press.

Kaplan, M. (1983). A woman's view of *DSM–III. American Psychologist, 38,* 786–792. http://dx.doi.org/10.1037/0003-066X.38.7.786

Kayser, K. (2005). Enhancing dyadic coping during a time of crisis: A theory-based intervention with breast cancer patients and their partners. In T. A. Revenson, K. Kayser, & G. Bodenmann (Eds.), *Couples coping with stress: Emerging perspectives on dyadic coping* (pp. 175–194). Washington, DC: American Psychological Association. http://dx.doi.org/10.1037/11031-009

Kayser, K. (2007). *The yin and yang of dyadic coping: Chinese couples coping with breast cancer.* Paper presented at the International Meeting on Close Relationships and Health, Vancouver, British Columbia, Canada.

Kayser, K., Cheung, P. K., Rao, N., Chan, Y. C., Chan, Y., & Lo, P. H. Y. (2014). The influence of culture on couples coping with breast cancer: A comparative analysis of couples from China, India, and the United States. *Journal of Psychosocial Oncology, 32,* 264–288. http://dx.doi.org/10.1080/07347332.2014.897292

Kayser, K., & Scott, J. (2008). *Helping couples cope with women's cancers: An evidence-based approach for practitioners.* New York, NY: Springer.

Kayser, K., & Sormanti, M. (2002a). A follow-up study of women with cancer: Their psychosocial well-being and close relationships. *Social Work in Health Care, 35,* 391–406. http://dx.doi.org/10.1300/J010v35n01_04

Kayser, K., & Sormanti, M. (2002b). Identity and the illness experience: Issues faced by mothers with cancer. *Illness, Crisis, & Loss, 10,* 10–26. http://dx.doi.org/10.1177/1054137302010001003

Kayser, K., Sormanti, M., & Strainchamps, E. (1999). Women coping with cancer: The impact of close relationships on psychosocial adjustment. *Psychology of Women Quarterly, 23,* 725–739. http://dx.doi.org/10.1111/j.1471-6402.1999.tb00394.x

Kayser, K., Watson, L., & Andrade, J. (2007). Cancer as a "we-disease": Examining the process of coping from a relational perspective. *Families, Systems, & Health, 25,* 404–418. http://dx.doi.org/10.1037/1091-7527.25.4.404

Kazlow, F. (2002). *Comprehensive handbook of psychotherapy* (Vol. 3). New York, NY: Wiley.

Keats, J. (1987). Letter to "my darling brothers." In R. Gittings (Ed.), *The letters of John Keats.* Oxford, England: Oxford University Press. (Original letter dated 1818)

Kilbourne, J. (1999). *Deadly persuasion: Why women and girls must fight the addictive power of advertising.* New York, NY: Free Press.

King, M. L., Jr. (1967, April 4). *Beyond Vietnam*. Retrieved from http://kingencyclopedia.stanford.edu/encyclopedia/encyclopedia/enc_beyond_vietnam_4_april_1967/

Kiselica, M., Englar-Carlson, M., & Horne, A. (Eds.). (2008). *Counseling troubled boys: A guidebook for professionals*. New York, NY: Routledge.

Klein, M., & Riviere, J. (1953). *Love, hate and reparation*. London, England: Hogarth Press.

Knudson-Martin, C., Huenergardt, D., Lafontant, K., Bishop, L., Schaepper, J., & Wells, M. (2015). Competencies for addressing gender and power in couple therapy: A socio emotional approach. *Journal of Marital and Family Therapy, 41*, 205–220. http://dx.doi.org/10.1111/jmft.12068

Koehn, C. V. (2010). Relational approach to counseling women with alcohol and other drug problems. *Alcoholism Treatment Quarterly, 28*, 38–51. http://dx.doi.org/10.1080/07347320903436185

Kohut, H. (1984). *How does analysis cure?* Chicago, IL: University of Chicago Press.

Kopala, M., & Keitel, M. (Eds.). (2003). *Handbook of counseling women*. New York, NY: Sage.

Kopala, M., & Keitel, M. (Eds.). (2017). *Handbook of counseling women* (2nd ed.). Thousand Oaks, CA: Sage.

Koss-Chioino, J. (2007). Book review: Judith V. Jordan, Maureen Walker, & Linda M. Hartling (Eds.), The complexity of connection: Writings from the Stone Center's Jean Baker Miller Training Institute. *Transcultural Psychiatry, 44*, 689–694. http://dx.doi.org/10.1177/13634615070440041004

LaBrie, J. W., Thompson, A. D., Ferraiolo, P., Garcia, J. A., Huchting, K., & Shelesky, K. (2008). The differential impact of relational health on alcohol consumption and consequences in first year college women. *Addictive Behaviors, 33*, 266–278. http://dx.doi.org/10.1016/j.addbeh.2007.09.010

Laing, K. (1998). Katalyst leadership workshop. Presented at "In Pursuit of Parity: Teachers as Liberators," Boston, MA.

Land, T., Chan, P., & Liang, B. (2014). Depression and relational health in Asian American and European American college women. *Psychology in the Schools, 51*, 493–505. http://dx.doi.org/10.1002/pits.21758

Larsson, M., Pettersson, C., Skoog, T., & Eriksson, C. (2016). Enabling relationship formation, development, and closure in a one-year female mentoring program at a non-governmental organization: A mixed-method study. *BMC Public Health, 16*, 179. http://dx.doi.org/10.1186/s12889-016-2850-2

Lenz, A. S. (2014). Integrating relational-cultural theory concepts into supervision. *Journal of Creativity in Mental Health, 9*, 3–18. http://dx.doi.org/10.1080/15401383.2013.864960

Lenz, A. S. (2016). Relational-cultural theory: Fostering the growth of a paradigm through empirical research. *Journal of Counseling & Development, 94*, 415–428. http://dx.doi.org/10.1002/jcad.12100

Lenz, A. S., Speciale, M., & Aguilar, J. V. (2012). Relational-cultural therapy intervention with incarcerated adolescents: A single-case effectiveness design. *Counseling Outcome Research and Evaluation, 3*, 17–29. http://dx.doi.org/10.1177/2150137811435233

Lerner, H. (1985). *The dance of anger.* New York, NY: Harper Collins.

Lerner, H. (2013). Helping remarried couples survive stepkids. In J. V. Jordan & J. Carlson (Eds.), *Creating connection: A relational-cultural approach with couples* (pp. 225–238). New York, NY: Routledge.

Levant, R. (1992). Toward the reconstruction of masculinity. *Journal of Family Psychology, 5*, 379–402. http://dx.doi.org/10.1037/0893-3200.5.3-4.379

Levant, R., & Pollack, W. (1995). *A new psychology of men.* New York, NY: Basic Books.

Levant, R. F., & Powell, W. A. (2017). The gender role strain paradigm. In R. F. Levant & Y. W. Wong (Eds.), *The psychology of men and masculinities* (pp. 15–44). Washington, DC: American Psychological Association.

Lewis, H. (Ed.). (1987). *The role of shame in symptom formation.* Hillsdale, NJ: Erlbaum.

Liang, B., Spencer, R., Brogan, R., & Corral, M. (2008). Mentoring relationships from early adolescence through emerging adulthood: A qualitative analysis. *Journal of Vocational Behavior, 72*, 168–182. http://dx.doi.org/10.1016/j.jvb.2007.11.005

Liang, B., Taylor, C., Williams, L., Tracy, A., Jordan, J., & Miller, J. (1998). *The relational health indices: An exploratory study* (Paper No. 293). Wellesley, MA: Wellesley Center for Women.

Liang, B., Tracy, A., Glenn, C., Burns, S., & Ting, D. (2007). The relational health indices: Confirming factor structure for use with men. *Australian Community Psychologist, 19*, 35–52.

Liang, B., Tracy, A., Kauh, T., Taylor, C., & Williams, L. (2006). Mentoring Asian and Euro-American college women. *Journal of Multicultural Counseling and Development, 34*, 143–154. http://dx.doi.org/10.1002/j.2161-1912.2006.tb00034.x

Liang, B., Tracy, A., Kenny, M., & Brogan, D. (2008). Gender difference in the relational health of youth participation in a social competency program. *Journal of Community Psychology, 36*, 499–515. http://dx.doi.org/10.1002/jcop.20246

Liang, B., Tracy, A. J., Kenny, M. E., Brogan, D., & Gatha, R. (2010). The relational health indices for youth: An examination of reliability and validity aspects. *Measurement and Evaluation in Counseling and Development, 42,* 255–274. http://dx.doi.org/10.1177/0748175609354596

Liang, B., Tracy, A., Taylor, C. A., & Williams, L. (2002). The relational health indices. *American Journal of Community Psychology, 30,* 271–288. http://dx.doi.org/10.1023/A:1014637112531

Liang, B., Tracy, A., Taylor, C. A., Williams, M., Jordan, J. V., & Miller, J. B. (2002). The relational health indices: A study of women's relationships. *Psychology of Women Quarterly, 26,* 25–35. http://dx.doi.org/10.1111/1471-6402.00040

Liang, B., & West, J. (2011). Relational health, alexithymia, and psychological distress in college women: Testing a mediator model. *American Journal of Orthopsychiatry, 81,* 246–254. http://dx.doi.org/10.1111/j.1939-0025.2011.01093.x

Liang, B., Williams, L. M., & Siegel, J. A. (2006). Relational outcomes of childhood sexual trauma in female survivors: A longitudinal study. *Journal of Interpersonal Violence, 21,* 42–57. http://dx.doi.org/10.1177/0886260505281603

Lieberman, M. (2013). *Social: Why our brains are wired to connect.* New York, NY: Crown.

Lipsky, S. (1987). *Internalized racism.* Seattle, WA: Rational Island.

Lombardi, K. S. (2011). *The mama's boy myth: Why keeping our sons close makes them stronger.* New York, NY: Penguin.

Magnavita, J. (2004). *Handbook of personality disorders: Theory and practice.* New York, NY: Wiley.

Maley, M. E. (2007). *The relationship between relational health and depression and social anxiety in college students* (Doctoral dissertation). Retrieved from OCLC WorldCat. (Publication 164437639)

Malik, K. P. (2013). Motherhood and marriage: Naming the work. In J. V. Jordan & J. Carlson (Eds.), *Creating connection: A relational-cultural approach with couples* (pp. 149–165). New York, NY: Routledge.

Markey, R. (2013). Strangers in a strange land: Men in relational couples therapy. In J. V. Jordan & J. Carlson (Eds.), *Creating connection: A relational-cultural approach with couples* (pp. 131–148). New York, NY: Routledge.

Markoff, L., & Cawley, P. (1996). Retaining your clients and your sanity: Using a relational model of multisystem case management. In B. L. Underhill & G. Finnegan (Eds.), *Chemical dependency: Women at risk* (pp. 45–65). New York, NY: Haworth Press. http://dx.doi.org/10.1300/J034v06n01_03

Markus, H., & Kitayama, S. (1991). Culture and the self: Implications for cognition, emotion and motivation. *Psychological Review, 98,* 224–253. http://dx.doi.org/10.1037/0033-295X.98.2.224

McIntosh, P. (1980, July/August). White privilege: Unpacking the invisible knapsack. *Peace and Freedom,* 10–12.

McIntosh, P. (1988). *White privilege and male privilege: A personal account of coming to see correspondences through work in women's studies* (Report No. 189). Wellesley, MA: Wellesley Center for Women.

McMillan, C. (2011). *What the body stories of girls tell us about autonomy and connection during adolescence* (Doctoral dissertation). Theses and Dissertations (Comprehensive). Retrieved from http://scholars.wlu.ca/etd/1088

McMillan-Roberts, K. D. (2015). *The impact of mutuality in doctoral students and faculty mentoring relationships* (Doctoral dissertation). Retrieved from ERIC. (Publication ED567339)

McWhirter, E. H., Valdez, M., & Caban, A. R. (2013). Latina adolescents' plans, barriers, and supports: A focus group study. *Journal of Latina/o Psychology, 1,* 35–52. http://dx.doi.org/10.1037/a0031304

Melles, E. A., & Frey, L. L. (2014). "Here, everybody moves": Using relational cultural therapy with adult third-culture kids. *International Journal for the Advancement of Counseling, 36,* 348–358. http://dx.doi.org/10.1007/s10447-014-9211-6

Mental health: Does therapy help? (1995, November). *Consumer Reports, 734–739.*

Mereish, E. H., & Poteat, V. P. (2015). The conditions under which growth-fostering relationships promote resilience and alleviate psychological distress among sexual minorities: Applications of relational cultural theory. *Psychology of Sexual Orientation and Gender Diversity, 2,* 339–344. http://dx.doi.org/10.1037/sgd0000121

Merzenich, M. (2000). Cognitive neuroscience. Seeing in the sound zone. *Nature, 404,* 820–821. http://dx.doi.org/10.1038/35009174

Miller, J. B. (Ed.). (1973). *Psychoanalysis and women.* Baltimore, MD: Penguin.

Miller, J. B. (1976). *Toward a new psychology of women.* Boston, MA: Beacon Press.

Miller, J. B. (1985). *The construction of anger in women and men* (Work in Progress No. 4). Wellesley, MA: Stone Center for Developmental Services and Studies, Wellesley College.

Miller, J. B. (1986). *Toward a new psychology of women* (2nd ed.). Boston, MA: Beacon Press.

Miller, J. B. (1989). *Connections, disconnections and violations* (Work in Progress No. 33). Wellesley, MA: Stone Center for Developmental Services and Studies, Wellesley College.

Miller, J. B. (2002). *How change happens: Controlling images, mutuality and power* (Work in Progress No. 96). Wellesley, MA: Stone Center for Developmental Services and Studies, Wellesley College.

Miller, J. B. (2003). *Telling the truth about power* (Work in Progress No. 100). Wellesley, MA: Stone Center for Developmental Services and Studies, Wellesley College.

Miller, J. B. (2008a). How change happens: Controlling images, mutuality and power. *Women & Therapy, 31*, 109–127. http://dx.doi.org/10.1080/02703140802146233

Miller, J. B. (2008b). Telling the truth about power. *Women & Therapy, 31*, 145–161. http://dx.doi.org/10.1080/02703140802146282

Miller, J. B., Jordan, J. V., Stiver, I., Walker, M., Surrey, J., & Eldridge, N. (1997). *Therapists' authenticity* (Work in Progress No. 8). Wellesley, MA: Stone Center for Developmental Services and Studies, Wellesley College.

Miller, J. B., & Stiver, I. (1997). *The healing connection: How women form relationships in therapy and in life.* Boston, MA: Beacon Press.

Mirkin, M. P. (1990, July). The new alliance: Adolescent girls and their mothers. *The Family Therapy Networker,* 36–41.

Mirkin, M. P. (1992). Female adolescence revisited: Understanding girls in their sociocultural contexts. *Journal of Feminist Family Therapy, 4*, 43–60. http://dx.doi.org/10.1300/J086v04n02_03

Mirkin, M. P. (1998). The impact of multiple contexts on recent immigrant families. In M. McGoldrick (Ed.), *Revisioning family therapy: Multicultural systems theory and practice.* New York, NY: Guilford Press.

Mirkin, M. P., & Geib, P. (1999). Consciousness of context in relational couples therapy. *Journal of Feminist Family Therapy, 11*, 31–51. http://dx.doi.org/10.1300/J086v11n01_02

Mirkin, M. P., & Geib, P. (2013). When 1+1 does not equal 2: The impact of context on couples therapy. In J. V. Jordan & J. Carlson (Eds.), *Creating connection: A relational-cultural approach with couples* (pp. 23–44). New York, NY: Routledge.

Mitchell, S. (1988). *Relational concepts in psychoanalysis.* Cambridge, MA: Harvard University Press.

Montgomery, M., & Kottler, J. (2005). The developing counselor. In D. Comstock (Ed.), *Diversity and development: Critical contexts that shape our lives and relationships* (pp. 91–111). Belmont, CA: Brooks/Cole.

Moore, R. C. (2011). *Close friendship between Black women and White women in the US: Fostering connection in a culture of disconnection* (Doctoral dissertation). Retrieved from ProQuest Information & Learning. (UMI No. 3474074)

Morray, E. B., & Liang, B. (2005). Peace talk: A relational approach to group negotiation among Arab and Israeli youths. *International Journal of Group Psychotherapy, 55*, 481–506. http://dx.doi.org/10.1521/ijgp.2005.55.4.481

Motulsky, S. L. (2010). Relational processes in career transition: Extending theory, research and practice. *The Counseling Psychologist, 38*, 1078–1114. http://dx.doi.org/10.1177/0011000010376415

Munson, M. R., Smalling, S. E., Spencer, R., Scott, L. D., Jr., & Tracy, E. (2010). A steady presence in the midst of change: Nonkin natural mentors in the lives of older youth exiting foster care. *Children and Youth Services Review, 32*, 527–535. http://dx.doi.org/10.1016/j.childyouth.2009.11.005

Myerson, D. E., & Fletcher, J. K. (2000, January/February). A modest manifesto for shattering the glass ceiling. *Harvard Business Review*, 127–136.

Nabar, K. K. (2011). *Individualistic ideology as contained in the* Diagnostic and Statistical Manual of Mental Disorders Fourth Edition Text Revision *personality disorders: A relational cultural critique* (Doctoral dissertation). Available from ProQuest Information and Learning. (Publication 3420997)

Neff, K. (2011). *Self-compassion: The proven power of being kind to yourself.* New York, NY: Harper Collins.

Norcross, J. (Ed.). (2002). *Psychotherapy relationships that work: Therapist contribution and responsiveness to patient.* New York, NY: Oxford University Press.

Norcross, J. C., VandenBos, G. R., & Freedheim, D. K. (Eds.). (2010). *History of psychotherapy: Continuity and change* (2nd ed.). Washington, DC: American Psychological Association.

Oakley, A., & Addison, S. (2005). *Outcome evaluation of a community-based mental health service for women employing a brief feminist relational-cultural model.* Paper presented at Jean Baker Miller Research Colloquium, Wellesley College, Wellesley, MA.

Oakley, M. A., Addison, S. C., Piran, N., Johnston, G. J., Damianakis, M., Curry, J., . . . Weigeldt, A. (2013). Outcome study of brief relational-cultural therapy in a women's mental health center. *Psychotherapy Research, 23*, 137–151. http://dx.doi.org/10.1080/10503307.2012.745956

Ossana, S., Helms, J. E., & Leonard, M. M. (1992). Do "womanist" identity attitudes influence college women's self-esteem and perceptions of environmental bias? *Journal of Counseling & Development, 70*, 402–408. http://dx.doi.org/10.1002/j.1556-6676.1992.tb01624.x

Pack, M. (2009). Clinical supervision: An interdisciplinary review of literature with implications for reflective practice in social work. *Reflective Practice, 10*, 657–668. http://dx.doi.org/10.1080/14623940903290729

Packnett, G. D. (2010). *In their voices: Retaining African American students at a predominantly White university* (Doctoral dissertation). Retrieved from http://irl.umsl.edu/cgi/viewcontent.cgi?article=1489&context=dissertation

Paris, R., & Dubus, N. (2005, January). Staying connected while nurturing an infant: A challenge of new motherhood. *Family Relations, 54*, 72–83. http://dx.doi.org/10.1111/j.0197-6664.2005.00007.x

Paris, R., Gemborys, M., Kaufman, P., & Whitehill, D. (2007). Reaching isolated new mothers: Insights from a home visiting program using paraprofessionals. *Families in Society: The Journal of Contemporary Social Service, 88,* 616–626.

Patton, J., & Reicherzer, S. (2010). Inviting Kate's authenticity: Relational cultural theory applied in work with a transsexual sex worker of color using the competencies for counseling with transgender clients. *Journal of LGBT Issues in Counseling, 4,* 214–227. http://dx.doi.org/10.1080/15538605.2010.524846

Pedersen, P., Crethar, H., & Carlson, J. (2008). *Inclusive cultural empathy: Making relationships central in counseling and psychotherapy.* Washington, DC: American Psychological Association. http://dx.doi.org/10.1037/11707-000

Penzerro, R. M. (2007). Review of diversity and development: Critical contexts that shape our lives and relationships. *Journal of Ethnic & Cultural Diversity in Social Work: Research & Practice, 15,* 173–175.

Pickering, B. J. (2014). Picture me different: Challenging community ideas about women released from prison. *Canadian Journal of Counseling and Psychotherapy, 48,* 270–283.

Pipher, M. (1994). *Reviving Ophelia.* New York, NY: Putnam.

Pleck, J. (1981). *The myth of masculinity.* Cambridge, MA: MIT Press.

Pollack, W. (1998). *Real boys: Rescuing our sons from the myths of boyhood.* New York, NY: Random House.

Porges, S. W. (2011). *The polyvagal theory: Neurophysiological foundations of emotions, attachment, communication and self-regulation.* New York, NY: Norton.

Portman, T. A., & Garrett, M. T. (2005). Beloved women: Nurturing the sacred fire of leadership from an American Indian perspective. *Journal of Counseling & Development, 83,* 284–291. http://dx.doi.org/10.1002/j.1556-6678.2005.tb00345.x

Protivnak, J. J., & Foss, L. L. (2009). An exploration of themes that influence the counselor education doctoral student experience. *Counselor Education and Supervision, 48,* 239–256. http://dx.doi.org/10.1002/j.1556-6978.2009.tb00078.x

Purgason, L. L., Avent, J. R., Cashwell, C. S., Jordan, M. E., & Reese, R. F. (2016). Culturally relevant advising: Applying relational-cultural theory in counselor education. *Journal of Counseling & Development, 94,* 429–436. http://dx.doi.org/10.1002/jcad.12101

Putnam, R. (2000). *Bowling alone: The collapse and revival of American community.* New York, NY: Simon & Schuster. http://dx.doi.org/10.1145/358916.361990

Racker, H. (1953). *Transference and countertransference.* New York, NY: International Universities Press.

Rassiger, C. A. (2010). *Student–teacher relationships and academic success in at-risk Latino and Black middle school students* (Doctoral dissertation). Available from ProQuest Dissertations and Theses database. (UMI No. 3455591)

Resnick, M. D., Bearman, P. S., Blum, R. W., Bauman, K. E., Harris, K. M., Jones, J., . . . Udry, J. R. (1997). Protecting adolescents from harm. Findings from the National Longitudinal Study on Adolescent Health. *JAMA, 278,* 823–832. http://dx.doi.org/10.1001/jama.1997.03550100049038

Robb, C. (1988, October 16). A theory of empathy: The quiet revolution in psychiatry. *Boston Globe Magazine,* p. 13.

Robb, C. (2006). *This changes everything: The relational revolution in psychology.* New York, NY: Picador.

Robinson, T., & Ward, J. (1991). A belief in self far greater than anyone's disbelief: Cultivating resistance among African American female adolescents. In C. Gilligan, A. G. Rogers, & D. Tolman (Eds.), *Women, girls and psychotherapy: Reframing resistance* (pp. 87–103). New York, NY: Harrington Park Press. http://dx.doi.org/10.1300/J015V11N03_06

Rock, M. (1997). *Psychodynamic supervision.* Northvale, NJ: Aronson.

Rogers, C. (1951). *Client-centered therapy: Its current practice, implications and theory.* Boston, MA: Houghton Mifflin.

Rogers, C. (1980). *A way of being.* Boston, MA: Houghton Mifflin.

Root, M. (1992). Reconstructing the impact of trauma on personality. In L. S. Brown & M. Ballou (Eds.), *Personality and psychopathology: Feminist reappraisal* (pp. 229–265). New York, NY: Guilford Press.

Rosen, W. (1992). *On the integration of sexuality: Lesbians and their mothers* (Work in Progress No. 56). Wellesley, MA: Stone Center for Developmental Services and Studies, Wellesley College.

Ruiz, E. (2012). Understanding Latina immigrants using relational cultural theory. *Women & Therapy, 35,* 68–79.

Safran, J., & Muran, J. (2000). *Negotiating the therapeutic alliance: A relational treatment guide.* New York, NY: Guilford Press.

Sagi, A., & Hoffman, M. (1976). Empathic distress in newborns. *Developmental Psychology, 12,* 175–176. http://dx.doi.org/10.1037/0012-1649.12.2.175

Sanftner, J. L., Cameron, R. P., Tantillo, M., Heigel, C. P., Martin, D. M., Sippel-Silowash, J. A., & Taggart, J. M. (2006). Mutuality as an aspect of family functioning in predicting eating disorder symptoms in college women. *Journal of College Student Psychotherapy, 21,* 41–66. http://dx.doi.org/10.1300/J035v21n02_06

Sanftner, J. L., Ryan, W. J., & Pierce, P. (2009). Application of a relational model to understand body image in college women and men. *Journal of College Student Psychotherapy, 23,* 262–280. http://dx.doi.org/10.1080/87568220903167182

Sanftner, J. L., & Tantillo, M. (2001). *A relational/motivational approach to treating eating disorders.* Paper presented at the Jean Baker Miller Training Institute Research Forum, Wellesley College, Wellesley, MA.

Sanftner, J. L., & Tantillo, M. (2004, June). *Development and validation of the Connection-Disconnection Scale to measure perceive mutuality in clinical and college samples of women.* Poster session presented at Jean Baker Miller Training Institute Research Forum, "Mutuality: The Interface Between Relationship and Culture," Wellesley College, Wellesley, MA.

Sanftner, J. L., & Tantillo, M. (2011). Body image and eating disorders: A compelling source of shame for women. In R. L. Dearing & J. P. Tangney (Eds.), *Shame in the therapy hour* (pp. 277–303). Washington, DC: American Psychological Association. http://dx.doi.org/10.1037/12326-012

Sanftner, J. L., Tantillo, M., & Seidlitz, C. S. (2004). A pilot investigation of the relation of perceived mutuality to eating disorders in women. *Women & Health, 39,* 85–100. http://dx.doi.org/10.1300/J013v39n01_05

Sassen, G. (2012). Drums and poems: An intervention promoting empathic connection and literacy in children. *Journal of Creativity in Mental Health, 7,* 233–248. http://dx.doi.org/10.1080/15401383.2012.711712

Schore, A. (1994). *Affect regulation and the origin of the self: The neurobiology of emotional development.* Hillsdale, NJ: Erlbaum.

Schumacher, A. (2014). Talking circles for adolescent girls in an urban high school: A restorative practices program for building friendships and developing emotional literacy skills. *SAGE Open, 4,* 1–13. http://dx.doi.org/10.1177/2158244014554204

Schwartz, H. L. (2010). *Thankful learning: A grounded theory study of relational practice between master's students and professors* (Doctoral dissertation). Retrieved from https://etd.ohiolink.edu/rws_etd/document/get/antioch1247833338/inline

Schwartz, H. L., & Holloway, E. (2012). Partners in learning: A grounded theory study of relational practice between master's students and professors. *Mentoring & Tutoring, 20,* 115–135. http://dx.doi.org/10.1080/13611267.2012.655454

Schwartz, H. L., & Holloway, E. (2014). "I become a part of the learning process": Mentoring episodes and individualized attention in graduate education. *Mentoring & Tutoring, 22,* 38–55. http://dx.doi.org/10.1080/13611267.2014.882604

Sears, W., & Sears, M. (2001). *Attachment parenting book: A commonsense guide to understanding and nurturing your baby.* New York, NY: Little Brown.

Seligman, M. (1991). *Helplessness.* New York, NY: Freeman.

Senghe, P. (1990). *The fifth discipline.* New York, NY: Doubleday.

Shannon, D. M. (2013). Gay male couple work: The value of individual and group therapy. In J. V. Jordan & J. Carlson (Eds.), *Creating connection: A relational-cultural approach with couples* (pp. 91–113). New York, NY: Routledge.

Sharf, R. (2008). *Theories of psychotherapy and counseling.* Belmont, CA: Thomson, Brooks/Cole.

Shem, S., & Surrey, J. (1998). *We have to talk: Healing dialogues between women and men.* New York, NY: Basic Books.

Shibusawa, T., & Chung, I. W. (2009). Wrapping and unwrapping emotions: Clinical Practice with East Asian immigrant elders. *Clinical Social Work Journal, 37,* 312–319. http://dx.doi.org/10.1007/s10615-009-0228-y

Siegel, D. J. (1999). *The developing mind: How relationships and the brain interact to shape who we are.* New York, NY: Guilford Press.

Siegel, D. J. (2010). *Mindsight: The new science of personal transformation.* New York, NY: Bantam.

Sifneos, P. E. (1979). *Short-term dynamic psychotherapy: Evaluation and technique.* New York, NY: Plenum Press. http://dx.doi.org/10.1007/978-1-4684-3530-6

Simner, M. (1971). Newborn's response to the cry of another infant. *Developmental Psychology, 5,* 136–150. http://dx.doi.org/10.1037/h0031066

Singh, A. A., & Moss, L. (2016). Using relational-cultural theory in LGBTQQ counseling: Addressing heterosexism and enhancing relational competencies. *Journal of Counseling & Development, 94,* 398–404. http://dx.doi.org/10.1002/jcad.12098

Skerrett, K. (2013). Resilient relationships: cultivating the healing potential of couples' stories. In J. V. Jordan & J. Carlson (Eds.), *Creating connection: A relational-cultural approach with couples* (pp. 114–130). New York, NY: Routledge.

Skerrett, K. (2016). WE-ness and the cultivation of wisdom in couple therapy. *Family Process, 55,* 48–61. http://dx.doi.org/10.1111/famp.12162

Skerrett, K., & Fergus, K. (Eds.). (2015). *Couple resilience: Emerging perspectives.* New York, NY: Springer. http://dx.doi.org/10.1007/978-94-017-9909-6

Sommers, C. (1994). *Who stole feminism?* New York, NY: Simon & Schuster.

Sormanti, M., & Kayser, K. (2000). Partner support and changes in relationships during life-threatening illness: Women's perspective. *Journal of Psychosocial Oncology, 18,* 45–66. http://dx.doi.org/10.1300/J077v18n03_04

Sparks, E. (1999). *Against the odds: Resistance and resilience in African American welfare mothers* (Work in Progress No. 81). Wellesley, MA: Stone Center for Developmental Services and Studies, Wellesley College.

Sparks, E. (2009). Learning to be authentic with clients: The untold journey of a relational practitioner. In A. Bloomgarden & R. Mennuti (Eds.),

Psychotherapist revealed: Therapists speak about self-disclosure in psychotherapy (pp. 163–179). New York, NY: Routledge/Taylor & Francis Group.

Spencer, R. (2006). Understanding the mentoring process between adolescents and adults. *Youth & Society, 37,* 287–315. http://dx.doi.org/10.1177/0743558405278263

Spencer, R. (2007). "I just feel safe with him": Emotional closeness in male youth mentoring relationships. *Psychology of Men & Masculinity, 8,* 185–198. http://dx.doi.org/10.1037/1524-9220.8.3.185

Spencer, R., Jordan, J., & Sazama, J. (2004). Growth-promoting relationships between youth and adults: A focus group study. *Families in Society, 85,* 354–362. http://dx.doi.org/10.1606/1044-3894.1496

Spencer, R., & Liang, B. (2009). "She gives me a break from the world": Formal youth mentoring relationships between adolescent girls and adult women. *The Journal of Primary Prevention, 30,* 109–130. http://dx.doi.org/10.1007/s10935-009-0172-1

Spiegel, D. (1991). A psychosocial intervention and survival time of patients with metastatic breast cancer. *Advances, 7,* 10–19.

Stein, D. (2010). Relational cultural theory: A feminist critique of human development and its implications for the practice of psychoanalytic psychotherapy. *Australasian Journal of Psychotherapy, 29,* 136–161.

Stern, D. (1986). *The interpersonal world of the infant.* New York, NY: Basic Books.

Stiver, I. P., Rosen, W., Surrey, J., & Miller, J. B. (2008). Creative moments in relational-cultural therapy. *Women & Therapy, 31,* 7–29. http://dx.doi.org/10.1080/02703140802145631

Stolorow, R., & Atwood, G. (1992). *Contexts of being.* Hillsdale, NJ: Analytic Press.

Striepe, M. I. (2013). Evolving sexualities for the couple: Interacting RCT and the sexual health model. In J. V. Jordan & J. Carlson (Eds.), *Creating connection: A relational cultural approach with couples* (pp. 114–130). New York, NY: New Routledge.

Surrey, J. (1991). The relational self in women: Clinical implications. In J. Jordan, J. Surrey, & A. Kaplan (Eds.), *Women and empathy: Implications for psychological development and psychotherapy* (Work in Progress No 2). Wellesley, MA: Stone Center for Developmental Services and Studies, Wellesley College.

Surrey, J. (2005). Relational psychotherapy, relational mindfulness. In C. Germer, R. Siegel, & P. Fulton (Eds.), *Mindfulness and psychotherapy* (pp. 91–110). New York, NY: Guilford Press.

Surrey, J., & Eldridge, N. (2007). *Relational-cultural mindfulness.* Presentation at the Jean Baker Miller Training Institute Workshop, Wellesley College, Wellesley, MA.

Surrey, J., & Jordan, J. V. (2013). The wisdom of connection. In C. K. Germer & R. D. Siegel (Eds.), *Wisdom and compassion in psychotherapy: Deepening mindfulness in clinical practice* (pp. 163–175). New York, NY: Guilford Press.

Tantillo, M. (1998). A relational approach to group therapy for women with bulimia nervosa: Moving from understanding to action. *International Journal of Group Psychotherapy, 48,* 477–498. http://dx.doi.org/10.1080/00207284.1998.11491568

Tantillo, M. (2000). Short-term relational therapy for women with bulimia nervosa. *Eating Disorders: The Journal of Treatment & Prevention, 8,* 99–121. http://dx.doi.org/10.1080/10640260008251218

Tantillo, M. (2004). The therapist's use of self-disclosure in a relational therapy approach for eating disorders. *Eating Disorders, 12,* 51–73. http://dx.doi.org/10.1080/10640260490267760

Tantillo, M. (2006). A relational approach to eating disorders in multifamily therapy group: Moving form difference and disconnection to mutual connection. *Families, Systems, & Health, 24,* 82–102. http://dx.doi.org/10.1037/1091-7527.24.1.82

Tantillo, M., & Kreipe, R. (2011). Improving connections for adolescents across high-intensity settings for the treatment of eating disorders. In D. Le Grange & J. Lock (Eds.), *Eating disorders in children and adolescents: A clinical handbook* (pp. 199–222). New York, NY: Guilford Press.

Tantillo, M., & Sanftner, J. (2003). The relationship between perceived mutuality and bulimic symptoms, depression, and therapeutic change in group. *Eating Behaviors, 3,* 349–364. http://dx.doi.org/10.1016/S1471-0153(02)00077-6

Tantillo, M., & Sanftner, J. L. (2010a). Measuring perceived mutuality in women with eating disorders: The development of the connection–disconnection scale. *Journal of Nursing Measurement, 18,* 100–119. http://dx.doi.org/10.1891/1061-3749.18.2.100

Tantillo, M., & Sanftner, J. L. (2010b). Mutuality and motivation in the treatment of eating disorders. In M. Maine, B. Hartman McGilley, & D. Bunnell (Eds.), *Treatment of eating disorders: Bridging the gap between research and practice* (pp. 319–334). London, England: Elsevier. http://dx.doi.org/10.1016/B978-0-12-375668-8.10019-1

Tantillo, M., Sanftner, J., & Hauenstein, E. (2013). Restoring connection in the face of disconnection: An integrative approach to understanding and treating anorexia nervosa. In D. Le Grange & J. Lock (Eds.), *Eating disorders in children and adolescents: A clinical handbook* (pp. 199–219). New York, NY: Guilford Press. http://dx.doi.org/10.1080/21662630.2013.742980

Tantillo, M., Sanftner, J., Noyes, B., & Zippier, E. (2003, June). *The relationship between perceived mutuality and eating disorder symptoms for women beginning outpatient treatment*. Presented at the Eating Disorders Research Society Annual Meeting, Ravello, Italy.

Tatum, B. D. (1993). *Racial identity development and relational theory: The case of black women in white communities* (Work in Progress No. 63). Wellesley, MA: Stone Center for Developmental Services and Studies, Wellesley College.

Tatum, B. D. (1997). *"Why are all the black kids sitting together in the cafeteria?" And other conversations about race.* New York, NY: Basic Books.

Tatum, B. D., & Garrick Knaplund, E. (1996). *Outside the circle? The relational implications for white women working against racism* (Work in Progress No. 78). Wellesley, MA: Stone Center for Developmental Services and Studies, Wellesley College.

Taylor, S. E. (2002). *The tending instinct: Women, men and the biology of our relationships.* New York, NY: Henry Holt.

Taylor, S. E., Klein, L. C., Lewis, B. P., Gruenewald, T. L., Gurung, R. A., & Updegraff, J. A. (2000). Biobehavioral responses to stress in females: Tend-and-befriend, not fight-or-flight. *Psychological Review, 107,* 411–429. http://dx.doi.org/10.1037/0033-295X.107.3.411

Thomas, A., & Sillen, S. (1972). *Racism and psychiatry.* New York, NY: Brunner Routledge.

Tomkins, S. (1987). Shame. In D. Nathanson (Ed.), *The many faces of shame* (pp. 131–161). New York, NY: Guilford Press.

Trepal, H. C. (2010). Exploring self-injury through a relational cultural lens. *Journal of Counseling & Development, 88,* 492–499. http://dx.doi.org/10.1002/j.1556-6678.2010.tb00051.x

Trepal, H. C., Boie, I., & Kress, V. E. (2012). A relational-cultural approach to working with clients with eating disorders. *Journal of Counseling & Development, 90,* 346–356. http://dx.doi.org/10.1002/j.1556-6676.2012.00043.x

Trepal, H., Boie, I., Kress, V., & Hammer, T. (2015). A relational-cultural approach to working with clients with eating disorders. In L. H. Choate (Ed.), *Eating disorders and obesity* (pp. 425–441). Alexandria, VA: American Counseling Association. http://dx.doi.org/10.1002/9781119221708.ch18

Trepal, H., & Duffey, T. (2016). Everything has changed: An interview with Judy Jordan. *Journal of Counseling & Development, 94,* 437–441. http://dx.doi.org/10.1002/jcad.12102

Tucker, C., Smith-Adcock, S., & Trepal, H. C. (2011). Relational cultural theory for middle school counselors. *Professional School Counseling, 14,* 310–316. http://dx.doi.org/10.5330/PSC.n.2011-14.310

Turner, C. (1984). *Psychosocial barriers to black women's career development* (Work in Progress No. 15). Wellesley, MA: Stone Center for Developmental Services and Studies, Wellesley College.

Turner, C. (1987). *Clinical applications of the Stone Center theoretical approach to minority women* (Work in Progress No. 28). Wellesley, MA: Stone Center for Developmental Services and Studies, Wellesley College.

Turner, S. G., Kaplan, C. P., & Badger, L. W. (2006). Adolescent Latinas' adaptive functioning and sense of well-being. *Affilia, 21*, 272–281. http://dx.doi.org/10.1177/0886109906288909

Turner, S. G., Kaplan, C. P., Zayas, L., & Ross, R. E. (2002). Suicide attempts by adolescent Latinas: An exploratory study of individual and family correlates. *Child & Adolescent Social Work Journal, 19*, 357–374. http://dx.doi.org/10.1023/A:1020270430436

VandenBos, G. R. (Ed.). (2015). *APA dictionary of psychology* (2nd ed.). Washington, DC: American Psychological Association.

VandenBos, G. R., Meidenbauer, E., & Frank-McNeil, J. (Eds.). (2014). *Psychotherapy theories and techniques: A reader.* Washington, DC: American Psychological Association. http://dx.doi.org/10.1037/14295-000

van der Kolk, B. A. (1988). The trauma spectrum: The interaction of biological and social events in the genesis of the trauma response. *Journal of Traumatic Stress, 1*, 273–290. http://dx.doi.org/10.1002/jts.2490010302

Vicario, M., Tucker, C., Smith-Adcock, S., & Hudgins-Mitchell, C. (2013). Relational-cultural play therapy: Reestablishing health connections with children exposed to trauma in relationships. *International Journal of Play Therapy, 22*, 103–117. http://dx.doi.org/10.1037/a0032313

Walker, E. K. (2011). Risk and protective factors in mothers with a history of incarceration: Do relationships buffer the effects of trauma symptoms and substance abuse history? *Women & Therapy, 34*, 359–376. http://dx.doi.org/10.1080/02703149.2011.591662

Walker, M. (1999). *Race, self and society: Relational challenges in a culture of disconnection* (Work in Progress No. 85). Wellesley, MA: Stone Center Stone Center for Developmental Services and Studies, Wellesley College.

Walker, M. (2001). *When racism gets personal: Toward relational healing* (Work in Progress No. 93). Wellesley, MA: Stone Center Stone Center for Developmental Services and Studies, Wellesley College.

Walker, M. (2002a). *How therapy helps when culture hurts* (Work in Progress No. 95). Wellesley, MA: Stone Center for Developmental Services and Studies, Wellesley College.

Walker, M. (2002b). *Power and effectiveness: Envisioning an alternate paradigm* (Work in Progress No. 94). Wellesley, MA: Stone Center for Developmental Services and Studies, Wellesley College.

Walker, M. (2005). Critical thinking: Challenging developmental myths, stigmas, and stereotypes. In D. Comstock (Ed.), *Diversity and development:*

Critical contexts that shape our lives and relationships (pp. 47–67). Belmont, CA: Brooks Cole.

Walker, M. (2008a). How therapy helps when the culture hurts. *Women & Therapy, 31*, 87–105. http://dx.doi.org/10.1080/02703140802145979

Walker, M. (2008b). Power and effectiveness: Envisioning an alternate paradigm. *Women & Therapy, 31*, 129–144. http://dx.doi.org/10.1080/0270314080 2146266

Walker, M. (2011). What's a feminist therapist to do? Engaging the relational paradox in a post feminist culture. *Women & Therapy, 34*, 38–58. http://dx.doi.org/10.1080/02703149.2011.532689

Walker, M. (2013). Liberating voice and vulnerability: Relational-cultural perspectives on conflict in mixed race couples. In J. V. Jordan & J. Carlson (Eds.), *Creating connection: A relational-cultural approach with couples* (pp. 61–74). New York, NY: Routledge.

Walker, M., & Miller, J. (2000). *Racial images and relational possibilities* (Talking Paper 2). Wellesley, MA: Stone Center for Developmental Services and Studies, Wellesley College.

Walker, M., & Rosen, W. (Eds.). (2004). *How connections heal: Stories from relational-cultural therapy*. New York, NY: Guilford Press.

Walsh, M. (1997). *Women, men and gender: Ongoing debates*. New Haven, CT: Yale University Press.

Ward, J. (2016). *The fire this time: A new generation speaks about race*. New York, NY: Scribner.

Ward, J. V. (2000). *The skin we're in: Teaching our children to be emotionally strong, socially smart, spiritually connected*. New York, NY: Free Press.

Watson-Phillips, C. (2007). *Relational fathering: How fathering sons affects men's relational growth and development* (Unpublished doctoral dissertation). Lesley University, Cambridge, MA.

Wells, A. (2005). *Disconnections in grief and the grief of disconnection: A relational-cultural approach to understanding and working with grief and loss*. Practitioner Program Project. Wellesley, MA: Jean Baker Miller Training Institute, Wellesley College.

West, C. K. (2005). The map of relational-cultural theory. *Women & Therapy, 28*, 93–110. http://dx.doi.org/10.1300/J015v28n03_05

Westkott, M. C. (1997). On the new psychology of women: A cautionary view. In M. R. Walsh (Ed.), *Women, men & gender: Ongoing debates* (pp. 359–379). New Haven, CT: Yale University Press.

Williams, M., Teasdale, J., Segal, R., & Kabat-Zinn, J. (2007). *The mindful way through depression: Freeing yourself from chronic unhappiness*. New York, NY: Guilford Press.

Winnicott, D. W. (1963). The development of the capacity for concern. *Bulletin of the Menninger Clinic, 27*, 167–176.

Winnicott, D. W. (1997). *Playing and reality*. New York, NY: Basic Books.

Zayas, L. H., Bright, C. L., Alvarez-Sánchez, T., & Cabassa, L. J. (2009). Acculturation, familism and mother–daughter relations among suicidal and non-suicidal adolescent Latinas. *The Journal of Primary Prevention, 30*, 351–369. http://dx.doi.org/10.1007/s10935-009-0181-0

Index

About the Author

Judith V. Jordan, PhD, is the director of the Jean Baker Miller Training Institute and founding scholar at the Stone Center of Wellesley College. Dr. Jordan is an assistant clinical professor of psychiatry at Harvard Medical School. She and colleagues developed a relational model of human development and clinical practice (relational–cultural theory) that emphasizes the centrality of relationship in our lives. After graduating Phi Beta Kappa and magna cum laude from Brown University in Providence, Rhode Island, she earned her PhD in clinical psychology at Harvard University in Cambridge, Massachusetts, where she received special commendation for outstanding academic performance. She was the director of psychology training as well as the director of the women's studies program at McLean Hospital, a Harvard Teaching Hospital. For the past 20 to 30 years she has worked with Jean Baker Miller, Irene Stiver, and Jan Surrey on the development of what has come to be known as relational–cultural theory.

Dr. Jordan has published over 50 original reports, 30 chapters, coauthored three books, and edited or coedited two books. She is the recipient of the Massachusetts Psychology Association's Career Achievement Award for Outstanding Contribution to the Advancement of Psychology as a Science and a Profession and was also selected as the Mary Margaret Voorhees Distinguished professor at the Menninger School of Psychiatry and Mental Health Science in the spring of 1999. She received the annual psychiatric residents' Outstanding Teacher of the Year award at

McLean Hospital in Belmont, Massachusetts, and she is listed in Who's Who in America. Dr. Jordan was awarded an honorary Doctor of Human Letters in 2001 from New England College in Henniker, New Hampshire, with "utmost admiration for her contribution to science and the practice of psychology." In 2002, she received a Special Award from the Feminist Therapy Institute in recognition of outstanding contributions to the development of feminist psychology. Dr. Jordan received the 2010 Distinguished Psychologist Award from the Division of Psychotherapy of the American Psychological Association, which is given to only one psychologist in the United States and Canada each year in recognition of outstanding accomplishments and significant lifetime contributions to the field of psychotherapy.

Dr. Jordan is on the editorial board of the *Journal of Clinical Psychology: In Session* and the *Journal of Creativity and Mental Health*. She has written, lectured, and conducted workshops nationally and internationally on relational–cultural theory, women's psychological development, gender differences, mothers and daughters, mothers and sons, empathy, mutuality, psychotherapy, shame, connections and disconnections, mutual empathy, marginality, diversity, courage, vulnerability, new models of strength, competence and connection, women's sexuality, gender issues in the workplace, marginalization, relational practice in the workplace, new models of leadership, traumatic disconnections, good conflict, competition and a relational model of self. Dr. Jordan frequently serves as a resource for researchers and the media on these issues; she appeared on the Oprah Winfrey show as an expert on the importance of relationships for personal and societal well-being.

About the Series Editors

Jon Carlson, PsyD, EdD, ABPP, is the distinguished professor of Adlerian psychology at Adler University, Chicago, and a psychologist with the Wellness Clinic in Lake Geneva, Wisconsin. Dr. Carlson is also professor emeritus at Governors State University in the Division of Psychology and Counseling, University Park, Illinois. He is a fellow of the American Psychological Association (APA), the American Counseling Association, and the Wisconsin Psychology Association. Dr. Carlson has written 62 books, over 180 articles and book chapters, and created over 300 professional training videos that are being used in universities and training centers around the world. Dr. Carlson has served as the editor of several periodicals including the *Journal of Individual Psychology* and *The Family Journal*. He holds diplomates in both family psychology and Adlerian psychology, received a Certificate of Psychotherapy from the Alfred Adler Institute (now Adler University), and received the Lifetime Contribution Award from the North American Society of Adlerian Psychology. He received the Distinguished Psychologist Award (Lifetime contribution to psychotherapy—APA Division 29, Society for the Advancement of Psychotherapy) and the 2011 Distinguished Career Contributions to Education & Training Award from APA. He is the coauthor (with Matt Englar-Carlson) of *Adlerian Psychotherapy*, which is part of the Theories of Psychotherapy Series.

Matt Englar-Carlson, PhD, is a professor of counseling and the director of the Center for Boys and Men at California State University–Fullerton.

He is a fellow of the American Psychological Association. As a scholar, teacher, and clinician, Dr. Englar-Carlson is focused on training clinicians to work more effectively with their male clients across the full range of human diversity. He has over 50 publications and 75 national and international presentations, most of which are focused on men and masculinity, social justice and diversity issues in psychological training and practice, and theories of psychotherapy. Dr. Englar-Carlson coedited the books *In the Room With Men: A Casebook of Therapeutic Change*; *Counseling Troubled Boys: A Guidebook for Professionals*; *Beyond the 50-Minute Hour: Therapists Involved in Meaningful Social Action*; and *A Counselor's Guide to Working With Men*, and was featured in the APA-produced DVD *Engaging Men in Psychotherapy*. He was named Researcher of the Year, Professional of the Year, and received the Professional Service award by the Society for the Psychological Study of Men and Masculinity. As a clinician, Dr. Englar-Carlson has worked with children, adults, and families in school, community, and university mental health settings. He coauthored (with Jon Carlson) *Adlerian Psychotherapy*, which is part of the Theories of Psychotherapy Series.